Writing in Stone

Tiny Keepsake Moments

First Published in 2023

Copyright 2023

All rights reserved. This book or any portion thereof may not be reproduced or used in any manner whatsoever without express written permission of the publisher except for the use of brief quotation in a book review.

Printed in the United States of America

First Printing September 2023

Cover Photo: Joe Zunker

Introduction

Each year at Christmas I write a touching story sent as a Christmas letter. I was tempted to not include these stories here and then I remembered the day my Christmas Story about Maggie's dog Oreo, arrived at their home in AZ.

Why do I remember that day?

Because I was on Facetime with Maggie when she opened it. I watched her face light up as she read the Oreo story for the very first time. With a massive smile she looked at the collage of pictures that were enclosed. She knew that 150 people on my Christmas card list had received this story – and many of them would be talking to her about her story.

Later she showed me that she kept the story at the back of her school notebook for safe keeping ... Oreo was a treasure for her and so was the story – a written memory of love.

That is when I decided to include the Christmas Stories that have been written each year since my last book. So, if a story is signed with love from Cathy and Joe, you will know that it was printed as it appeared in our annual Christmas story letter.

Authentically me ...

"I think with each book I become more authentically ME" I said to my twin sister. She sounded surprised by my comment and asked, 'What do you mean?'

"Well, when I wrote my first book there were people who were miffed that I had not come out and called the story something mystical – that some of the magic of a story was left hidden and the reader had to fill in the blanks. In this 3rd book I am more true to myself, letting the real me show ... the person that I am becoming ... "

I think this makes Carol curious. I think that's funny! The person who has known me every second of my life ... might be curious about knowing me! That makes me laugh!

Hoping that your own precious stories come bubbling up, as you read mine.

Cathy

Dedication

" Write your Sad times in Sand,

Write your Good Times in Stone."

George Bernard Shaw

I have a place in my heart for good and beautiful things ... that space is claimed permanently by the people who have given me beautiful stories to write ...

To Joe

To my sons John, Rob and Tom.

To my daughters-by-choice, Shannon and Brittany

To my grandchildren Brady, Maggie, Cameron, Tatum, Taylor, and Lexi

Writing in Stone

Tiny Keepsake Moments

By Cathy Weber-Zunker

Florida Keys..8

When there were Two & When there were Three...11

Cookies..15

Conversation with Strangers.........................18

Delores..21

Did you bring mints?....................................26

Don't Do That...31

Caught in the Act...35

Brady's Wisdom...39

Blackbirds...42

Drivers Exam...44

Betting on Us...49

Enough for Everybody..................................52

Best mistake..57

Favorite Customer.......................................60

Being the Hero..63

Alone By Myself...67

Foresight	72
Free session	73
Welcoming Tatum	77
I Can Take Him Anywhere	83
Water Puddle	87
Gifts of the heart	91
Twin Stories	95
God in My Office	99
The Rocking Chair	103
Grand Daughters	108
The Oak Chest	110
Hammertime	114
The Lighter	117
Hugging John	119
The Lamp	123
Hummer	126
The Closet	129
Hunting Rabbit	133
Tatum's Hand	137
Invasion of Privacy	140
Tatum's Conversation	141
Just One More Thing	144
Tate's Hearing	148
The Knife	151
Take Your Shoes Off	156

Laura My Bunny Lady................................159
Surprise Surprise Surprise!......................168
Lemonade Stand......................................173
Superhero..176
Like a Good Neighbor...............................178
Substitutions...183
Line in the Water......................................186
Spilled Soup..190
Little Yellow Dress....................................192
Slow Slow Slow...195
Lost Car..199
Hero Day..203
Love Lifts us Up..208
Rob's Friends...211
LuLu..213
You paid Last Time..................................216
Most Beautiful Blanket.............................219
Red Firebird...224
Mr. Swanson..227
Rebecca...230
Legacy Plants..235
Pity Party...238
Nibbling Ears...241
Pillow Time..244
Of Course!...247

Pheasant for Lunch... .249

Oreo Christmas.. 254

Overtime.. 258

Searching for Gabriel............................. 265

Gummy Worms..272

Welcoming Taylor..276

Post it Notes...279

On My Lap...283

Maggie's World..287

Leave Wanting More...292

Like Father Like Son...297

The Tree...302

Meeting Bill Heegaard..308

Permissions

Florida Keys
2017

It was like a cartoon, the ones you watched as a kid. Our boat was speeding across the water when suddenly the water was gone. We were beached on the soft sand. The accidental beaching onto land was as soft as setting a sleeping baby in a cradle. If there were guidelines for accidentally and gently beaching a boat, this sea captain would have won the prize. We were in no physical danger whatsoever. No one was hurt. The boat didn't seem to be damaged. It wasn't a joke. No one was laughing. Off in the distance we could see 7 Mile Bridge spanning the big water. We were simply at a complete stop, on a tropical sandbar in the Florida Keys with the sun setting. We were stranded in the big water. If I had to pick my cartoon character – I was Pluto, staying in the background, at the back of the boat.

We had come here to laugh together and vacation but no one was laughing now . We were here in this predicament because we were trying to grab for everything; for MORE. We insisted on taking a sunset cruise instead of sitting quietly on the rocks, we had to reach for more than the beauty that was right in front of our rented home. Those chairs at the end of the dock ... the ones with seagulls flying overhead ... the sun was rising in the morning and the very same sun setting at night ... not once, not one person, including myself, went to the rocks to sit in the Adirondack chairs there. They didn't look soft ... they didn't look cushy, and so we made our way up the dock to the comfortable pool and sitting area right outside the house. Sitting on manmade smooth concrete instead of watching the seagulls from the uncomfortable rocks.

In the middle of our hurry to have the perfect vacation ... this evening, nature itself stopped us ... dead in our tracks ... out in the middle of nowhere ... with the quiet of the ocean all around ... giving us exactly what we came here seeking.

Peace, quiet and harmony.

And still we missed it. Instead of stopping to see what we came here for, everyone was pushing and striving now to get OUT of the quiet ... to get unstuck from the sandbar. To get out quickly before we are discovered for exactly what we are ... driving a boat under the influence of "never having enough". You know ... that drug ... the one that doesn't let us walk calmly anywhere – until the sun finally sets without us noticing it setting once again.

We were looking for MORE ocean and MORE sunset and MORE excitement and we certainly got more than we bargained for! That same drug that brought us out here in the big water, because we were not content to sit quietly on land and enjoy the view – we had to have more.

In the chaos we radioed for assistance and the cavalry was on the way to rescue us. With all the pandemonium going on around me ... I sat there completely unnoticed at the back of the boat ... it was then that I heard a small voice quietly say, "Look up."

"What?" I thought.

And then ...

The voice repeated "Look up!"

I did ...

I looked up ... from one side of the horizon all the way across to the other side of the horizon ... as far as I could see up into the sky ... slowly the sky began to glitter with stars ... the vastness of sky, now meeting the vastness of water as the water started sparkling like diamonds. The sun was setting and the line that separates the sky from water was fading with the light ... minute by minute it was happening ... soon the tapestry of darkness now backlit the stars. **This is exactly what I had come here for.** I almost missed it. I sat there mesmerized by the half sphere ,all by myself at the back of the boat, watching the upside down bowl of fading light.

The best words I heard all day ...

all week ...

all year ...

came from within, "Look up".

When There Were Two

1 14 2020

I claimed my own room.

Well, not really.

They just gave me a room because I just showed up looking like a lost puppy dog waiting at the door to be let in. It's a pathetic sight.

My expression says, "Can I come in and play for a while? Maybe stay overnight? I just happen to have a change of clothes with me!"

It was on one of these nights in Fargo, as I crawled into bed under my electric blanket that had been preheated for hours – I found myself wondering when the day would come, the very FIRST time those two little ones would come down to wake me up. They both could manage the steps now. Sometimes little Tatum needed some help.

I crawled into bed that very night and the next morning I was meditating in the still darkness. There was just the glow of footlights that followed the steps downstairs. Even with my eyes closed I saw the light beam go dark for just a moment, and I opened my eyes.

What I saw coming down the steps was Brittany in exercise clothes, holding the hand of little Tatum. I heard Tatum's wee little voice say 'Gamma go? Gamma go?' Where did grandma go?

While momma exercised, Cam and Tatum and I read stories in the fort in the basement.

When There Were Three

Children's books with hidden pictures!!! What a great idea! Shine a flashlight behind each page and the kids were interested in the books for ... about five minutes. Seriously... that is how long it took to get completely bored with the books.

The real toy was the flashlight. My grandmother Facebook post read "Don't bother buying toys, just buy a flashlight ... give it to a four-year-old ... a three-year-old and an almost two year old, take them downstairs to the basement ... shut off the lights and have hours of fun!

That's what we did. In the dark playing 'real'.

I have no idea where the kids came up with that word. Playing 'real' describes a game with flashlights in the basement, shutting off the lights. Big grandpa Joe is sitting on the couch covered with a blanket in the dark while the kids approach his mummy-looking body on the sofa. As they creep toward the scary monster covered with the blanket ... they are holding flashlights as they approach. When the timing seems right, the big grandpa sits up like a monster and makes a **roar**!

Screams of delight come from the semi-darkness as all three children with flashlights come running across the basement floor to safety. After the burst of scary excitement, Grandpa Joe returns to his quiet sofa and pulls the blanket over his head once again and the game of 'real' begins again. I watch to make sure everyone was safe and no one was scared for real and the game went on until bath time.

"We have to stay overnight!" later Joe insisted to me.

"**That's the best part!** When the kids come down to wake us up in the morning!"

The next morning Joe and I lay in our basement bedroom hearing the patter of feet on the main floor above. We know that those three little munchkins are up and surely they are asking to come downstairs to wake us up. Their momma is monitoring them and telling them to wait until she thinks it's an appropriate time for all three of them to come down and climb into bed with us.

Maybe our Daughter-in-law doesn't know that Joe and I are just as excited as they are ... the kids waiting upstairs and the grands waiting downstairs ....

Soon we hear the voice of a little girl say "grandpa Doe (Joe) whe (where) a' (are) oo (you)" ... the ends of the words trail off in the cutest most absolutely adorable fashion, wanting to know where her grandpa is.

Three ... all toddling downstairs at the same time. Three little kids are so thrilled that Grandma and Grandpa were in the spare bedroom downstairs.

As I lay in the darkness, the foot lights on the steps of the softly carpeted staircase, is muted through my closed eyelids and so is my mind. I'm not sure if Joe is sleeping or if he is awake and pretending sleep like I am.

Here we are on a Sunday morning, throwing back the covers of our bed and saying "Come on in!"

They joyously jump into bed with the two of us. Cameron and Tatum easily getting onto the bed and Taylor needing a boost to get up. And we talk and laugh and great big strong grandpa Joe lifts and twirls them around as if they weighed nothing at all. That is why they come!

They are thrilled that big strong grandpa is lifting them and turning them upside down. We will hug you and kiss you and love you for as long as you can handle it ... until you scream for mercy and beg for freedom ... because we love you that much. The kisses don't end ... and the smiles are perpetual ... and the sky is always blue when we are with you.

And finally, the novelty wears off and it's time to get up ... we wish it could last all day ... Grandpa Joe's magic of welcoming the day ... no wonder he insists on staying overnight ... it truly IS the BEST part of the day!

Cookies

3 20 2020 In Minnesota

"NO I don't want my money back!" I said to the UPS representative. I suggested that perhaps I should NOT have written 'COOKIES' on the shipping label – perhaps I should have lied. The representative at the other end of the conversation was aghast at what I was insinuating! Yes, I **was** absolutely suggesting that an employee took and ATE my shipment.

I was pissed off! All I wanted was a taste-of-home for my kids and grands in Arizona to have cookies from MN. It is NOT ok to piss me off! I didn't want the 16 bucks back and they didn't bother refunding it.

****

In Arizona

A full year later, I was talking with Maggie on Facetime, and she told me everything at her home in Phoenix was normal EXCEPT that she saw a lady walking down the street, taking something OUT of every mailbox.

In the background I heard Maggie's dad holler, "Maggie where's my phone? Some lady is stealing mail out of the mailboxes"

The lady stealing Christmas mail went on to another house to take mail out of the box. She had a big black Purse that she was putting the mail into, and her driver was sitting in a car waiting."

I remembered that one of their neighbors across the street was an FBI agent.

Then the woman went to the next house, which belongs to a police officer. She went to three mailboxes in the neighborhood while Maggie's brother Brady was taking pictures of the car, but didn't get the license plate.

Maggie's dad yelled at the lady and she saw him running out of the house toward her, so she hopped into the getaway SUV that was waiting for her and took off going down the street. John grabbed his car keys and started going around and around the blocks trying to find the culprit. As he spun around the block he found the criminal's car waiting in a left-hand turn lane. They were stuck there - blocked by traffic and had to wait. Another driver was aware of what was going on and had pulled up and took pictures of the car, the people, and the license plate.

All the information was submitted online; the neighborhood FBI agent also called it in; and 45 minutes later two police officers came to Maggie's house and there was a conversation between the FBI agent, neighborhood police officer, and my son.

I wondered if the lady stealing the mail was the one who ate my cookies last year.

As Mags told me the story, I realized that a year ago I may have jumped the gun – accusing UPS of stealing and eating my box of cookies.

I might owe UPS an apology.

I was just so disappointed after spending the time making the individualized cookies and carefully packing them so they would arrive intact ... and then shipping them overnight so they would get there fresh – and my level of disappointment was larger than my compassion for a company that I thought was the cause of my disappointment.

Tomorrow is just an ordinary day in April. And maybe it would be a great day to bake and send some cookies to my kids in Arizona. A surprise when no one is expecting cookies. And maybe, someday ... I will just hop on an airplane and deliver them unannounced ... homemade cookies delivered to their door ... by their own mother ... now that would be ... delivery at its finest!!!!

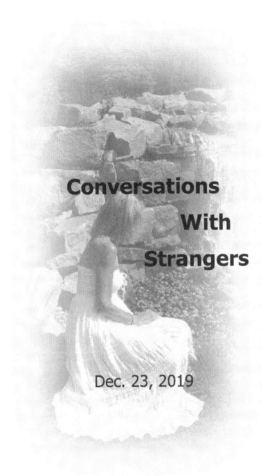

Conversations With Strangers

Dec. 23, 2019

Two days before Christmas Wal Mart was crazy busy!!

I was standing in front of the Ritz crackers, waiting for bottlenecked shoppers to pass by. I needed the crackers for my green bean/corn casserole for Christmas.

There was a gray-haired man that came by, and our eyes met. There is something disarming about looking someone in the eyes. Ever since the man behind me at Aldi's told me that he had just been diagnosed with cancer … that was when I knew that the angels were asking for a quick favor … just a few minutes of my time please.

Since that day, I try to not EVER rush past people in a store. I believe too much in the angels bringing people together and I don't want to miss the moment.

I said hello to the man. He was tall man with gray hair, and he started talking about something mundane. He said something about all the people in the store.

He chatted for a moment and as he got closer, he said "I've been an over the road trucker most of my life and I met a lot of people who are not very good; but there were some good ones too. And I can tell that you're one of the good ones."

And I thanked him for the compliment and then with his head hanging down he said, "This is kind of a hard time of year for me. My wife died two years, five months, and 14 days ago". Now he moved to the side of the aisle so that the flock of other people could pass by. I said to him, "I'm so sorry for your loss" and he said 'thank you' with a surprised look on his face.

I knew he was surprised that I used those words, because after two years, five months and 14 days, I'm sure that everyone else assumes that he should be over it by now.

He said that they had been married for 61 years, and she had been in a care facility for over three years. Once again, he said the exact number of years, months and days that she was in a nursing facility ... and he went to see her twice a day ... every day.

There was so much grief and loss inside this man, had we been alone, he would have sat down and wept. He talked about his wife and what a wonderful woman she was. She had worked for years for their church and then after that she went to work for a Dr. and worked side by side with the Physician. So proud of her he was!

I asked how old he was, and he said that he was 84, but he didn't look like it, not by any means.

Before we parted I went into my purse to get a Christmas letter. I always write a touching story as our holiday letter and without knowing why, that morning I had put a couple of extra copies in my purse. I gave it to him; he didn't seem surprised. When we said goodbye, I reached around him and gave him a hug. He looked startled and grateful.

About 10 minutes later I saw him in another aisle of the store. I was stunned at how different he looked now! He didn't look tall anymore and he didn't look solid right now – his face was pale and it looked as if it was even a struggle pushing the cart. As if that heavy weight had been easier to carry 10 minutes ago, while we were talking, and now by himself it was overbearing, too intense, too strong, to even attempt a smile.

He had used up all of today's energy to tell me about the hurt and the loss and now the hurt and the loss were winning. He had told me ... just one person ... about his beautiful wife and her accomplishments ... and that was enough for today. Hopefully, tomorrow he would find someone new ... who would just take a moment to hear about a woman who had been so spectacular ... so magnificent that his world revolved around her ... for 61 years while she was here on Earth ... plus two years, five months, and 14 days ... since she has been gone.

Delores

Thanksgiving was coming and it was my responsibility to bring the dressing. Patty, my sister-in-law, asked me to make it with raisins. "You know", she said "like your mom used to make".

Delores, my mom, had been gone for nearly twenty years. During these 20 years, I have grown into myself and as I grow, I realize I have learned more from my mother since she's been gone, than I did while she walked the earth. I understand her more. I have more compassion for her life experience now.

My mom, Delores, was a housewife-looking-woman, light complexion, slightly curly hair that nearly covered her ears—she was somber and serious looking. Delores is not a common name, so when I meet someone with that name, I pay attention.

****

One day several years ago, an inquiring woman called for a hypnosis appointment and specifically wanted to know if I could do Quantum Healing Hypnosis Technique. I had never heard of it. I had to look it up on the Internet. The client wanted someone who specialized in this particular technique.

I went to my computer, not my iPad, not my phone, ... to the full size computer screen searching for Quantum Healing Hypnosis Technique - and I waited for the screen - yes, in real time, waiting with the slow Internet connection. (High speed fiber optic cable will be installed just days from now, before Christmas)

As the page opened, the face of a woman appeared on the screen.

She was a housewife-looking-woman, light complexion, slightly curly hair that nearly covered her ears—she was somber and serious looking. The woman on the screen could've been my mother. Her name was Delores.

This unassuming woman had written 19 books and spoken around the world. There was not a doubt in my mind that I had to study this technique.

Even though this Delores no longer walked the Earth, I was able to study directly under her watchful eyes. Her entire training series had been recorded, as if you were sitting directly in front of her in the classroom. It felt like she was talking straight to me. So, I studied, allowing the legacy of another Delores to lead me along my path.

****

A few weeks ago, I was taking a nonstop flight from the small town of St Cloud, Minnesota to Arizona. A few other travelers and I were way too early. Security personnel had not even arrived at the small regional airport yet and no ticket agents staffed the counters. There was a young woman walking hurriedly with a suitcase and I said "Well, I guess we are early!" and the woman said, "Yeah I guess so!" and briskly proceeded to the lady's room, as if there was a waiting line or a reason to hurry.

There was nothing to do but pick a chair and wait. So, I sat next to an elderly woman.

She was a housewife-looking-woman, light complexion, slightly curly hair that nearly covered her ears—she was somber and serious looking. The woman could have been my mother.

Her story was one of loving and losing her first husband. Then, loving and losing her second husband all with the glow of happy memories and gratitude. We had a lot of time to talk. She was not self-absorbed. After telling many stories, she asked about my life. I told her that my wonderful husband was hunting today, and he actually got a deer that very morning before I left home. Her face lit up "Oh! I'm so glad you love your husband! So many don't."

She was concerned about going through security having had two knee replacements. She was alone by herself with a big suitcase. We had been visiting well over 30 minutes, when a ticket agent arrived. I had already printed my ticket - but my new friend had not - so I helped her gather her things before we went to go get her ticket. As she got out of her chair I said, "I'm Cathy".

She casually said, "I'm Delores."

I froze for a moment ... and then said "Well, Delores, it's so nice to meet you!" Now I knew ... I had been brought to the airport early to give her a hand and to keep her company.

We got her ticket and the woman at the counter told her she would have to pay extra for the crocheting bag as a second piece of luggage, unless she found room for it in her purse or suitcase. The two of us went around the corner and she was trying to put her purse inside the crochet bag or vice versa but neither was working. Finally, working with the pouches on the outside of her suitcase, which were already full, I took each piece from her crochet bag and individually laid out each piece flat inside the already overstuffed suitcase. Using some gentle persuasion, we zipped the suitcase.

I was through security quickly as I had been issued a ticket with TSA pre check. I stood there watching as the security agents scanned Delores' knees and went through her purse.

The two of us split up after security, but from a distance I watched her like a hawk - making sure she was OK. And if I couldn't see her for a few minutes, I would scan the small airport boarding area until I found Delores.

As I got on the airplane, I saw that she was neatly settled in her seat.

Pondering this latest Delores...took me back. I sat quietly on the airplane, talking with no one ... pondering thoughts of my mother.

I still make my mom's Gritwurst recipe (a breakfast sausage made from pork, cinnamon and steel cut oats) ... and I make cake donuts from scratch ... and yes, I made the dressing for Thanksgiving.

I don't pretend that my dressing is the caliber of my mother's stuffing. But mine is close enough ... to take us all back ... back to the old kitchen... back to a time when life was easy but we didn't' know it ... back to a time when we had all the answers to the wrong questions.

The food takes us back to our time together ... growing up and laughing.

The food takes us back to a time of ...   eating and playing together once again ...

The food takes us back ... to our mom ... Delores.

"Did You Bring Mints?"

"Did you bring mints for the kids?" Joe asked as we left the driveway heading for Tom and Brittany's lake cabin.

"Of course!" I said.

The containers get refilled and repacked immediately after each visit. Each time we are together, it doesn't take long before a little voice echoes the same question Joe had just asked, "Grandma, did you bring mints?"

It started when Cameron was a toddler, and discovered a box of mints in my purse that made a jingling sound. The container fit perfectly in his little pocket and rattled with each step. He could pull it out, take out a candy treat and then put it back in his pocket. He loved it so much, I got him his own container and put just a few little mints inside each visit. He would carry it around in his little big boy jeans pocket until the mints were gone and then return the empty container to me, for next time.

This little game became a regular part of each visit ... Cameron would ask, "Grandma, did you bring mints?" The answer was always 'yes' ... then Tatum and Taylor joined the game as they grew into toddlers themselves. Now, this coming weekend, little one-year- old Lexi will be receiving her first container filled with baby yogurt morsels.

Joe's question had jogged a memory from a long time ago, that surprised even me. I started to tell Joe a story ... something that I had never mentioned, nor thought of at all, in our decades together.

I said, "My parents had a friend named Jim when I was a little girl. All I know is what I saw and overheard about him. Jim wore shoes like none I had ever seen before. The shoes were made of leather, and were perfectly formed to his malformed feet; constructed because he had lost some toes. I had heard my parents talk about Jim fighting in a war, getting shot and that Jim still had shrapnel in his body. Even though it wasn't spoken, the assumption was that this middle-aged man would never get married because of his injuries. He owned the little grocery store in the small town of Morton, Minnesota."

I continued, "Rose was a lifelong friend of my mom's and Rose's husband had died. She was a jovial and outgoing woman and lived in the small town of Morton, MN. Since my mom's first husband had died (Jerry, Pat and Mary's dad) I assumed that the two women may have befriended each other because of loss, but I honestly don't know. I never knew any of the details about her situation, but Rose was a widow, and she knew that she would never get married again."

"Jim and Rose became travel companions and I often wondered if this caused people in a small town to talk or gossip about them. But all the years that I knew them, it seemed as though they were an old married couple, out for a Sunday afternoon drive, coming to our house to visit."

I would hear someone say, "Jim and Rose are coming!" We knew that the house was going to be filled with great 'catching up on all the old hometown news' as they would visit with my mom and dad.

My twin sister and my brother and I were excited too! Jim and Rose brought us candy from the grocery store! We rarely ever got candy from a grocery store! So, it was a big deal! We never knew what the sugary treat might be, it was always a surprise!

One time, when we were in Morton, we got to be inside Jim's grocery store when it was closed to the public! We thought he was rich! That one special day... he let us choose a candy item from his store ... for free! Anything we wanted!

And then one day I heard the words once again, "Jim and Rose are coming to visit!" I waited filled with excitement! Maybe they would bring something new that I had never seen before!

They got out of the car greeting everyone and going with mom and dad into the kitchen to sit around the table to drink coffee and visit ... but that day ... for whatever reason ... there **was no candy**.

No one else seemed to notice. The day just went on as if it was a normal day. I had a sinking feeling of being forgotten, a feeling of deep disappointment.

I watched as they talked with Mom and Dad at the dining room table over coffee, hoping one of them would go apologetically to the car and bring candy in, but they didn't! I even inconspicuously walked by their car in the driveway hoping to see some unclaimed candy on the dash or on the front seat. Nothing.

Months went by until their next visit and I was still holding onto the hope that the previous time was just a fluke. Certainly, this time they would remember us ... certainly they would know ... and remember the game ... but they never brought candy again. I remember the disappointment ...

Maybe they decided we weren't kids anymore ... that we were too big for such treats ... maybe we were too old for such silly games ... I don't know, but still, I checked each time they came to visit ... they never brought candy again. I couldn't understand why the game had ended.

As Joe listened to my story, I could see him putting the pieces together as I concluded, "That is why, the mint containers are immediately refilled and packed back in my travel bag as soon as we get home."

I hadn't even realized this memory was lurking in the back of my mind. I couldn't believe that I was telling Joe about a disappointment that had happened decades ago ... and how much this affected me ... the game had ended without warning or explanation. And now in the car the story was tumbling out of my mouth, like something that was urgent to be told.

Joe listened quietly as the story ended; I said, "I'm going to take mints to my grandchildren every time ... until the day that no one asks."

The end of the story just hung there in the car.

I love Jim and Rose for being a part of our lives. And they stopped bringing treats when they felt the time was right. But it taught me a lesson that I hadn't even realized was in the back of my brain. **I am not going to end the game** ...

Every time they ask "Did you bring mints?" I will say 'yes' ... until the day that they forget to ask ... the day that the mints will be forgotten by the children. And on that day , I'm not going to say a word.

The next visit I will pack the mints again, just to make sure that the game is really over.

I might shed a tear but I will be happy and satisfied knowing that I have fulfilled my objective ... four little grandchildren knowing ... that they are never forgotten ... not ever.

"Don't Do That"

Inside the big garden down at the bottom of our hill, Joe was going around and around on the four-wheeler. The garden down below our hill is fenced 8 feet high so the deer walk around it. Joe had a drag attached to the four-wheeler as he was leveling and pulverizing any chunks and lumps of soil. This lower garden grows the vegetables that take all summer to mature – the potatoes and squash – they are the plants that spread and need a lot of room!   I saw him down there in the sun on this marvelous summer day and I quickly abandoned whatever I had been doing.

I walked down the wide mowed trail that weaves its way behind Joe's shop, grateful for the warm season that was unfolding everywhere around us.   Joe paused the four-wheeler when he saw me. I was meandering down the hill with a big smile on my face while absorbing the abundant warmth of the sun.

"Wanna ride?" he hollered over the loud motor.

"Of course!" I hollered back

He got off to let me climb on behind him.

When he settled back in, I reached my arms around him more firmly than necessary, going around and around basking in the early summer sun with the clean fresh air and feeling the pure joy of being alive. Leaning into him, I said into his ear, "Don't do that!" and we laughed hilariously together!!!! He KNEW I was going to say that!

"Don't do that!" is grandparent speak – it comes from toddler cuteness – from a time when a toddler, (not just any toddler but OUR toddler grandchildren) said something so precious ... so insightful ... so rock bottom TRUE that you carry it with you forever.

"Don't do that" came out of little Cameron's (3 yrs.) mouth one day when he got up sleepily from his nap to discover that his daddy had mowed the grass at the lake cabin ... without him ... while he was sleeping. As he looked somberly at the already mowed lawn, he said to his daddy quietly, "Don't do that."

There it was: Wisdom in three small words. Don't do that FUN thing without ME nestled in your arms on the seat. "Don't do that" without my hands on the steering wheel too. "Don't do that" without me because I want the magic of the sunshine and the air and the noise all mixing together.

And you might think those innocent toddler perceptions would wear off or be forgotten by the grands ... but it does not disappear ... it's a grandparent secret ... we have a private treasure chest of the heart with a lock and key to save them forever.

Joe left a love note on the kitchen counter for me just a few days ago, for me to find when I got home at the end of the day. The sticky note said "I'm so glad **you** have **me**" with a smiley face and a heart on it. That 'wisdom moment' came from grandson Brady. (now 23) When Brady was a toddler, I had the delight of having him in my daycare. Every day when I got him out of his crib after his nap, I would hug him and say, "I'm so glad I have you!"

Then, one day, when I went to get him up from his nap, he leaned back in my arms and said to me, "I'm so glad **you** have **me**!" That was over 20 years ago ... and we still use those words of love.

"That is the bomb diggity!" was created by little Maggie. (now 16) When Maggie was small, she heard adults use the slang words 'that's the bomb.' So, if something was extraordinarily amazing, she would say, "THAT is the bomb diggity!' ... and all these years later ... Joe and I STILL use those words when something is outrageously wonderful.

So far ... Brady, Maggie and Cameron have graced us with words of wisdom that will last forever in our treasure chest of the heart. I can't know yet what profound thoughts we will gain from Little Miss Tatum (2 yrs.) and Little Miss Taylor (8 mos.) ... but I do know there is more to come .... and when it does ... we will tuck it away in our minds and hearts ... we are ready ... that treasure chest is nowhere near full yet ...

Leveling the garden on that magnificent Summer day ... the two of us together doing ordinary stuff ... arms and legs mashed together on the four-wheeler and a feeling inside of ... **"I'm so glad YOU have ME!"** on that "**bomb diggity**" summer day as I hollered above the motor noise, **"Don't do that"**...

This Christmas wishing you ... a treasure chest of the heart ... stuffed and overflowing ... with innocent wisdom

Cathy and Joe

Caught in the Act

Secret Santa and delivering May Baskets USED to be a big thing. Going through the neighborhood leaving a nameless gift at someone's door. The key was to be anonymous and not get caught.

Until today, I had never been caught, giving a gift like that. At least not that I know of. No one has called me on it. He is the only stranger who saw exactly what I was doing and said something about it.

It was just a little thing.

Another 16-year-old at the back entrance to the office building; with her father. She had paperwork in her hand and looked nervous.

I had my briefcase in one hand and a purse slung over my shoulder and a bag with lunch in it in the other hand. The young father next to his 16-year-old daughter opened and held the door for me on this pristine July day in Minnesota. I thanked him and said to his daughter, "Are you doing your driver's test today?"

She nodded 'yes'.

I turned toward her more directly and said, "I just want you to know that the examiners here are REALLY nice people. They are kind and they are always on your side. They want you to pass. So just relax and it's going to be fine."

I turned to go into the building as I have done hundreds of times before, when the young father with a twinkle in his smile, looked me straight in the eyes and said, "Thank you for that." As if to say "you didn't have to do that, but what a gift! " I nodded a 'you're welcome' nod and went on with my day.

I can't even count the number of times I have said these same words, to nervous teens to help them relax just a little bit, but this was the first time I felt SEEN so directly. Caught in the act ... of being a Secret Santa; giving the gift of words and encouragement. But Secret Santas aren't supposed to get found out ... clearly, I had gotten caught.

One day I saw a car returning to the driver's exam parking space. The young lady driving had dark skin and was wearing a sari. On the outdoor picnic table were three people waiting – two women in saree and one man – all the same complexion as the young lady testing. The young lady got out of the car and walked S L O W L Y, one deliberate step at a time behind the examiner toward the building. Each of her steps was slow and cautious, as she strode across the parking lot.

She saw me there, watching her.

As soon as the examiner stepped out of sight into the building, the slow walk and the composure was gone! At the picnic table she FLUNG herself into her dad's arms!!!! The two women gathered round and all of them were dancing in a circle around the young woman that succeeded today...

I put my window down with a HUGE smile on my face and gave her a thumbs up! I shouted "WooHoo!!!" She looked over at me and flung both her arms up with a thumbs up jumping up and down with excitement. It reminded me of a Rocky movie. She waved to me vigorously as I pulled out of the parking lot.

Once again, I was caught in the act ...

But it's not an act ... I want every single one of those nervous 'wanna be' teenage drivers to do their very best ... so they can pass GO on the monopoly board and move on to the next square. This is universal ... it crosses from one culture to another; from one human being to another ... we ALL want the very best for our children.

I am repeatedly saying the same words over and over ... day after day ... to someone else's child; because there were those nameless people who did it for me when I was growing up ...

there are those nameless people who did it for my sons as they were growing up ...

and I would be willing to bet that you ... the reader that is holding this book ... yes YOU ... right now; I bet you have a story that you could tell ... about someone that you helped namelessly ... and maybe you only told one single person about it ... and maybe you told no one. Because you are a part of a silent vast majority that is quietly willing to help others ... you are a part of the nameless population that has helped me and my sons and now my grandsons and granddaughters as they step forward in life.

We all know the power of positive words ... We all know the power of words from a stranger. Words from a person that has no skin in the game ... no ulterior motives ... just speaking the truth as they see it. So I use that power ... every single chance I get. This is my Secret Santa gift.

I already know what gift the teenager wants – they want to pass the test – so I help them out ... with words.

Most of the time it goes unnoticed ... but I like being nameless in the crowd; knowing that we are all in this together ... that people from around the world ... all want the same thing ... the very best for our children ... I was caught in the act for sure ... it costs me nothing ... to be a Secret Santa ... delivering words of encouragement ... Monday thru Friday ... all year long...

Brady's Wisdom

The last time I saw Brady face to face, I noticed it right away.

I didn't say anything about it, of course, that would not be polite.

There was a streak of white whiskers about half an inch wide going down into the youthful dark beard. It was at least an inch long and located on the left side of his mouth. The newly acquired distinguishing characteristic, was subtle and tasteful. But then everything about Brady is subtle and tasteful. His hair and beard are meticulous ... his manners, no matter where he goes, are always respectful ... he is an excellent conversationalist and if he says he's going to do something; he does it..

It had been a hard year for Brady, and as our family approached the upcoming weekend, I think all of us, Brady included, were happy to be focusing on something else. Still, I touched the streak of white whiskers as I kissed his face ... he lets me do that, because I'm his grandma.

This particular weekend in Arizona was designated for the celebration of our granddaughter's birthday. It was Maggie's time to shine and shortly after her birthday she would be graduating too! It was not going to be a time of discussing Brady's experiences.

However, I walked by the open door to his bedroom and saw him sitting on the corner of the bed. I walked into the room, crouched down in front of him and once again I stroked that white patch of whiskers in his beard.

And I said to him, "I know what this is Brady".

He looked at me quizzically and he said, "What is it?"

I said one word. "Wisdom".

He said to me "You're not the first person that's told me that".

It is a physical reminder of what he has gained through the past difficult year or two ... a sign of sorts that he has grown ... not a full beard of white but enough to remind him daily of the muck and the mire he has been through ... a telltale sign like a scar that is proudly displaying that it has healed the wound beneath it.

And there is plenty of normal colored beard left to be a canvas backdrop for future wisdom. The beard leaves lots of room and plenty of time for other challenges as time goes by. The speckles of gray will come in slowly now ...

leaving the white streak standing out Boldy until he slowly accumulates more wisdom.

The HARDEST turmoil in his life so far is in his past and that turmoil becomes the measuring stick for the rest of his life ... something to compare future obstacles to. Not many people have WORST events before the age of 25 ... not many are asked to stretch and grow in profound ways, at such a tender age.

But his beard will keep track of life as it unfolds for him. Keeping track of the lessons learned, organizing them into win/loss columns inside his own mind. Brady has depth beyond his years and I'm betting that he already knows that our ONLY losses are the events we choose not to learn from.

I hope he touches the white whiskers and can feel the difference in texture between the two colors ... because the white ones are much more valuable than the ones he was given by birthright. Brady has been changed forever, by the white ones.

I still don't say anything about the whiskers when I see him ... it's not my business ... but inside myself I smile every time ... proud of who he is becoming ... glad that he has the whiskers as a visible signature, like at the bottom of the Bill of Rights, the white streak authenticates what he has accomplished ... and when he looks in the mirror ... I hope he's proud of those whiskers ... and of himself.

Blackbirds

11 2 2017

It looked like a slick of black oil, across the entire roadway up ahead and down into the ditches on both sides as well. What was I seeing up ahead on the road?

I started to slow down, wondering if the nearly setting sun was playing tricks with my eyes. A solid black looking oil slick in Minnesota was a bit out of the ordinary. It was an unfamiliar sight to say the least. Then in the next moment the black started to move ... started to lift off the ground, like a tidal wave of water floating up into the sky. Birds! A massive tidal wave of small blackbirds.

I went from 55 miles an hour down to about 35 miles an hour, so that I wouldn't run any of them over. Over the course of 15 minutes there were two or three times I had to slow down for another flock of birds. I was driving on a two-lane county road, on my way to Fergus Falls to pick up my sons dogs. When I got to Fergus Falls, Tom quietly listened to my story. As he listened, I realized that there was no way for me to convey the magnitude of my experience. It was simply something you had to see for yourself.

There were thousands of black birds and they moved off the road almost like driving through water when the water sprays off to the side.

As the sea of birds was parting for me, I was grateful as I looked in my rear-view mirror, that there was a car behind me. I was just so glad that someone else witnessed this too ... it was a performance of nature that doesn't' happen in the city ... and I had no idea that it happened in the country either! It was just a quiet country road ... and wide-open spaces ... where the birds were free to sit by the thousands.

Whoever the other person was on the road, I hope they too took pause at the magic happening there. It has been five years since I had this experience. I wrote it down when I got home because I had never seen such a site before that day. In five years I have never seen such a site since ... and I doubt that I ever will again.

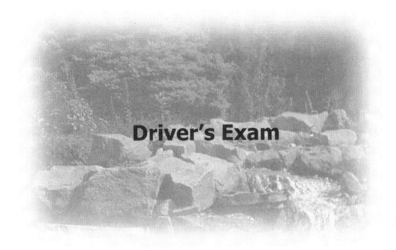

Driver's Exam

I saw it coming, before it happened. From a half block away, I saw the car at a complete stop at the cross street on my left. I was on a through street, I had the right of way.

As if without thinking, the driver pulled out in front of me. I was forced to come to a nearly complete stop as the other car entered the intersection. The car cut me off – plain and simple.

If this were the end of the story that would be fine with me. I am more than happy to give someone else the benefit of the doubt. I know for sure there have been times when others have given me the benefit of the doubt, and I appreciate it.

I followed the car slowly and to my surprise, in half a block the car turned right. Odd, I thought - we are both turning here and going the same direction.

In another half a block the car turned right once again. Odd I thought once again, they are turning into the parking lot – well isn't that interesting ... both of us pulling into my office parking lot – and then – the dawning awareness hit me! All the tumblers falling into place. "Oh Shit!" I hollered in the car – "Shit shit shit!!!!"

Even before I looked, I KNEW that the person who had cut me off was taking their drivers exam! They were returning to the government office, the Driver's Testing Station, located at the lower-level parking lot. Whoever was driving that vehicle had just failed their test. There was a sinking feeling in the pit of my stomach. I didn't know their name ... didn't know if they were male or female ... didn't know what race or creed ... but I do know, it was a 16-year-old who just an hour ago was filled with high hopes and excitement. I see it all the time – every weekday, in this parking lot.

As I walked from my car to the building, the examiner was now standing outside the car, talking through the driver's window to the young man behind the wheel. I heard the examiner say, "You've taken this test twice now. Now you need to spend a couple weeks practicing before you take the test again".

My head hung low as I went inside. A minute later, I returned to my car for something I had forgotten. Now the young man was in the passenger seat of the car with an adult, most likely his mother, driving him away. The young man looked straight ahead staring, not moving a muscle.

In this parking lot there is a full array of emotions all day long. There is nervousness, excitement, high hopes, disappointment, extreme distress ... a full array of parents and languages and skin colors and nationalities.

In this place ... it is all about parents supporting their kids. When I ask a parent "How are you?" as I enter the building, the most common response is "I'll let you know in 15 minutes". The parents are just as nervous and involved as the child.

One day I was leaving the parking lot on the "uphill" street that leaves our office. This hill is only dangerous if there is snow and ice covering it. But this day there was only sunshine and an inexperienced semi-truck driver taking a road test, probably nervous as heck. I was waiting at the stop sign on the 'uphill', when the inexperienced driver of the semi was about to make a left hand turn onto the residential street where I waited.

I knew it was someone that was testing, there would be no other reason for a semi-truck in this mostly residential area. The back end of the flatbed was unable to make the corner. Yes, with a nervous driver behind the wheel, the flatbed was about the sheer off the top half of my vehicle! "Oh shit!" I said talking out loud to myself. I put my car in reverse and started backing down the hill, allowing the truck to make the turn.

Later that afternoon as 4:30 approached, I stopped by the nearly empty driver's exam office. I peaked in the doorway as the examiners were finishing up end-of-day paperwork and asked, "So ... who was testing the semi driver?"

I just waited ... and waited ... for the three examiners to think ... and just let the question hang in the silence ... finally one of the examiners blurted out, "Was that YOU!?!" "Was that you on the street on the hill?" With a BIG smile I assured him it was me. He said "Well! Welcome to my world! At least three heart-stopping moments every day!" As he shook his head, I left the building smiling all the way to my car.

He's right, there ARE heart stopping moments happening all day long. But he thinks they are all happening during testing. In reality they are happening before, during and after ... all behind the scenes in the world of the parent and the child.

I know the parents are having heart stopping moments ... because ... I stop to ask. Sometimes just for a minute, offering an opportunity for someone, to tell me just a little bit more like ... their child doesn't really have a lot of experience driving and they are worried ... but they DID drive the whole two hours to the testing station today ... many say they are nervous for their child ... one parent said their child is handicapped and is testing for the fourth time and if they fail again, how will they survive the ride home?

Every time a look of gratitude crosses their face, that someone stopped ... to listen ... to care about the adult that stands BEHIND the child ... those people lifting the heavy beams of support for the teenager. I just let them know I'm on their side ... rooting for them and their child to be the ones going home today with loud celebration and excitement.

This building has two other parking lots I could use, but I choose to park here. I'd rather enter the building where REAL life is happening. I'm just freely passing out words of encouragement ... feelings of hope ... and helping someone smile.

But the child isn't going to know any of this for a long time ... the child doesn't know about parent's heart stopping moments ... holding their child's hopes and dreams in their hands ... keeping those hopes safely nestled and protected ... not wanting anything to go wrong for their child ...

I choose this parking lot so I can smile at parents ... nodding at mothers that are sitting alone ... so that with a knowing glance I can say "good luck", as I walk by. It might mean that once in a while I'm hollering "SHIT!" out loud in my vehicle ... I don't care ... I'd rather be in this parking lot ... where REAL life is happening.

Betting On Us

January 20, 2021

I started the betting.

It was a harmless thing to do during the boredom of a pandemic. Yes, we were using real money. $5 dollar bills ... sometimes $20.

Sitting around the fire cage in the back yard, on a cool desert Arizona evening and the comfort of family – those people that know you well and still love you.

We were betting on a most unlikely event ... a piece of wood ... a stick actually ... laying across the top frame of the circular firepit. Flames were licking at the stick and beginning to turn it black. I thought to myself ' I wonder when will it burn through the center? Hopefully both pieces will fall into the fire.'

As we sat in the dark with flames flickering, we were each lost in thought, each thinking in our own arena ... Rob good with mechanical processing; perhaps he was thinking about that. John good with engineering processing equipment; perhaps he was thinking about that. Maggie engineering her young future; perhaps she was thinking about that. Shannon accomplished at managing people; perhaps she was thinking about that ... and me ... lost in my own thoughts.

There's something about a fire in the middle of a group that changes everything. It's a place to let your eyes settle. There is room to say what's on your mind even if you haven't fully thought it through yet. Just broach a subject and see what the others think. It's safe ... to let yourself be real around a fire ... with these people.

We have something in common ... looking out for each other ... never doubting the inner strengths of each other ... we are spending three days talking of ambitions and aspirations. How could it be otherwise? It's a constant cycle in our heads. 'Where am I going? Does this feel right?' Five people all asking questions that can only be answered from within ... asking the important questions.

I looked across the top of the fire at John and said, "That's going to take five minutes to burn through and then drop into the fire."

John said, "No I don't think it's going to take that long."

And the betting began! The money came out and the whole vacation changed! We had ... a game!

There were those long silent periods around the fire ... when the stick was burning and when your mind was drifting back onto the earlier conversation; but now you can resume the earlier conversation because the other person is right there, to pick up with right where you left off just an hour ago. No need to call them back because we are all sitting around the fire.

When you hear someone else talking about what they are building in their life, you can't help but say, "I wonder what I could do?" I bet I could do a job like that ... I bet I could be thin and fit ... I bet I could be patient and kind.

The wheels in the mind keep on turning ... as the fire burned and as each new stick was laid on top, we bet again ... and the stakes are high in this family.

You may say, "What do you mean?" There is no bashing or downgrading of each other – there are no demeaning comments – no not at all – none to be sure. You may ask "If everybody is on your side , you've got it made! That is the ideal ultimate situation!"

But it is the opposite. There is so much love and support – there is so much positive and encouragement; hope and expectations are continually nudging and pushing you forward; and sometimes when you doubt yourself you **can't stop** – because there is a **whole group of others** who believe in you and see your success even more clearly than you do ...

Sometimes it would be easier to have others tell you that you can't do it – then you could STOP and let yourself be justified in a losing mentality ... you could blame or justify that somebody important to you was the CAUSE of your failure... but not in this family – the only way you are going to lose ... is to quit and give up on yourself. Nobody else in this family is going to give up on you ... not a chance ... because when the fire is lit ... and the betting begins ... in this family ... we always put our money ... on each other.

Enough For Everybody

The giant bubble was floating above the children about ten feet off the ground. It was changing shape as the warm summer breeze moved it. The rainbows in the bubble were mesmerizing in the sunlight. It disintegrated dropping a mist of clean smelling droplets onto the heads of the children as they giggled and scampered to make more.

"Doesn't **everyone** carry bubbles in their vehicle?" I certainly do! They are a hit no matter where I go. You may think that I bring them out only when children are around, but nothing could be further from the truth. The fabric bag, with a variety of giant bubble wands and a flat dish for dipping bubble wands is enticing for all ages.

I had packed for five days of taking care of little grandkids. They were going to be missing their parents, even though their parents would be just across town ... at the hospital ... having baby number four. My car was heavy with projects that children 5 and under would love, as well as my well-traveled bag of bubbles, located permanently on the floor behind the driver's seat in my car.

I had plenty of help for the weekend. Fun Grandpa Joe came for a while. Uncle Robbie, my second son, was on board entertaining and distracting them and bringing his own menagerie of toys and games. Even with lots of fun stuff we were all getting tired of waiting to meet this new baby girl, named Alexis.

In our impatience, we sat at the table doing a painting project, I said to big Uncle Robbie and the little kids ... "Let's put our intention out there to the universe, so that they can bring the baby home today!" We were tired of waiting – you could feel it in every one of us – why not just say it out loud?

Cameron, Tatum and Taylor followed along chanting with me ... "Come home today! Come home today!, Come home today! " ... just a little while later, we got a text message saying that they would be coming home TODAY!!

The house started going back to normal, as mom dad and baby nestled into their cozy home. Uncle Robbie gratefully went home to the quiet of his apartment.

The following day, while mom and dad and the new baby went back to have a checkup at the clinic, I took the three kiddos to the park to play. I packed the bag of bubbles at the bottom of the stroller. We hadn't used them the entire time yet, there were just so many other things to do.

Our trips to the park always start with swing time, but today the swings were full ... filled with a rainbow of colors, shapes, and sizes ... all nationalities and skin colors.

All three of the grandchildren ran to the slide!

Just a day earlier, Little Taylor saw a boy come running full speed to the slide. Instead of taking the STAIRS up, his tennis shoes got traction on the slide itself and went to the top. I've seen it hundreds of times before, but this was Taylor's moment of learning! It was as if her eyes and brain were analyzing every movement she had just seen.

She saw it once ...

She did it herself ... and nailed it!

Taylor never took the stairs up the slide again!!!!

With the swings still occupied I decided to get the bubbles out. We took them a little bit outside the playground, in the grassy area. Cameron crouched down getting the giant wands out of the bag. Turning, he saw the other children looking curiously over toward him. He went back to his job, untangling the strings of the giant bubble wands, getting out the trays, and pouring the bubble solution.

Giant bubbles were floating with the air currents above the park. Cameron turned around again and saw the curiosity of all the other children watching. Some of them hesitantly started moving in our direction.

Without a seconds pause Cameron turned his head and hollered "C'mon!"

He yelled again loudly, "C'mon!!! There's enough for everybody!"

And they came. ALL the children came. They all gathered around – there were hands and feet and questions everywhere ... they started picking up wands and bubble toys. There were little bubbles and big bubbles floating in the air across the playground.

I watched as Cameron managed the group and invited every child to come and play with his bubbles. The wands were passed around and all the kids wanted to try out the different shapes and sizes ... the plastic jars of soap, filled and refilled the trays.

When the bubble soap was all gone ... or spilled ... everyone was leaving cleaner than when they had arrived. The other children politely said thank you as the mothers asked questions about the recipe for giant bubbles.

 The playground was empty now ... we moved seamlessly to the swings ... continuing our chatter ... not admitting ... that the world had changed today ... the world became a better place today because of Cameron Joseph Weber.

There was only one place this little boy learned "C'mon! There's enough for everybody!" and that was at home. Cameron had welcomed everyone, no matter what size, shape or color, with his words "There's enough for everybody!".

I wanted to whisper 'thank you' in Cameron's ear, but he wouldn't have understood. He doesn't know that there are children in the world longing to have a playmate. He doesn't know that there are children in the world just wanting to be included. He doesn't realize that every act of inclusion ripples through the world ... making it better.

I think back to another older grandchild of mine. Maggie, like Cameron, welcomed everyone as she grew up ... taking a special needs boy to prom because she knew there was someone longing to be included. A gift basket for a special needs friend in the hospital ... because she knew that there was someone who needed her comfort.

Maggie too has made the world a better place. For Maggie it was bigger than bubbles ... because she is a little older ... she still includes everyone ... her innocence is just like Cameron. "C'mon! There's enough for everybody!"

At the park that day I could have invited all of those children myself ... with my adult wisdom and perspective ... but Cameron invited those children to play ... from his years of innocence.

My tears dried on my face in the sun ... pushing the stroller ... on our way home ... thinking about ... Maggie and Cameron.

Inclusion ...

... it's a

... Weber Thing

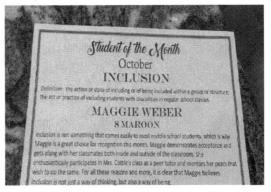

Best Mistake EVER

November 2020

It was the best mistake I ever made. I gave incorrect information from one son to another. You know how it is when you are the mom and you get to be the hub for family information ... the place where all the news gets dispensed; and I love it! Most of the time I get it right!

I had mentioned news to John, something about what was happening in Tom's business. I didn't realize that I had made a mistake. I really didn't!

When I saw Tom at our Thanksgiving celebration, he seemed a little bit irritated with me. I apologized immediately. He gave me all the details and kindly and properly set me straight. Due to the incorrect information, John had called Tom and said, "I don't often get a chance to be a big brother and give some advice" and to discuss the situation. All he wanted was for Tom to know that his older brother had his back.

Tom assured his older brother that he did NOT need any business help.

Yes, I'm smirking as I type this; laughing out loud actually!!!   Because none of my sons need help or advice with their work.

And me? I loved my response to this gentle reprimand. (I'm still smirking here)

I assured my son that there is ONE FOOLPROOF way to avoid such a misunderstanding in the future and that is ... drum roll ... **call your brother yourself!** Touché!

Realizing that I had just won this round of sparring, Tommy smiled a sheepish grin ... he knew I had a point – they woefully neglect their connection right now. For now, they are busy creating lives and making money and doing all the same things, I was doing at their age.

So, for now, I am the one at the center of the family wheel, holding them together. I love my place. I won't intentionally make a mistake again, but I will purposely encourage more conversation between the three of them.

I love that John picked up the phone, called Tom and is watching out for his younger brother. They don't know yet that they are going to need each other again. I didn't know it until my parents were aging and then gone. There will come a time when I'm gone, and they will RE-bond with each other; needing each other, more than they ever imagined.

There will be a time when they will pick up the phone; using some silly excuse of needing to ask something, just to hear the comfort of each other's voice. Or maybe they will get on an airplane to be together ... to hear the brother voices in person, that they heard through the years growing up ... the familiar sound of comfort ... going back ... to the way it felt a long time ago ...

... when they talked together in a teeny tiny bedroom

... talking about nothing and everything.

... planning what life would look like.

... they had each other's backs then ... and my best

mistake ever showed me unquestionably ....

that they still ... have each other's backs.

Favorite Customer

The woman behind the checkout counter was pointing out the grocery store app icon on my phone. I said to her apologetically, "SORRY! I just downloaded this app yesterday."

"I know" she said, " I helped you yesterday."

I was stunned! I looked around at five checkout lanes all bustling with a constant overflow of customers. I asked incredulously "How did you remember that?"

She said, "Because you are my favorite customer!"

WHAT? I thought!!! Why?

When I asked why I was her favorite customer she told me about a day **many months ago,** at the beginning of Covid 19 pandemic. I had completely forgotten about it.

She was not wearing a mask. It was in the deeply fearful part of the pandemic when there were no answers to any of the questions. Everyone was required to wear a mask unless they had a breathing issue. I remember looking at her and could see the discomfort on her face. She looked scared and fearful being the only one not wearing a mask. Hundreds of people moving through her lane each shift, perhaps even shoppers switching lanes not wanting to be near someone maskless.

I remember I said to her, "I'm so excited for you, that you don't have to wear a mask!" She looked shocked at my comforting comment.

She said "I'm feeling judged! I'm feeling like everyone is staring at me or pointing their finger at me like I'm a bad person!" I remember the look of relief that my comment brought to her face that day probably a year ago now.

I walked out of the store, her words still echoing in my mind ... I was still feeling stunned ... tears biting at the corners of my eyes.

The days of wearing masks are over now ... yet she still remembers me ... her favorite customer ... because the guidance system of the Universe – call it God or angels or energy – directed me to be in the **right** place at the **right** time to help someone else for the **right** reason ... in a way that I could not conceive.

The tears in my eyes and the question in my mind was; how often am I doing the bidding of the angels? And if I am **not listening;** do the angels need to turn to someone else?

If I'm in a pissy mood ... did I pass up opportunities that could have been mine to distribute encouragement? How many times have the angels sent someone else in my stead.

And, when I AM in a pissy mood, have the angels sent someone with words of encouragement to me ... have I gratefully accepted those words or rejected them?

It is no small thing to say a kind word ...   how many times can I look back in my life when someone said to me EXACTLY what I needed to hear at that moment? Like the checkout clerk at the grocery store, I may not remember the exact words, but I can tell **you how they made me feel.**

You just don't know what's really going on in someone else's life ... and that one little comment ... those kind caring words ... just might be the kiss of an angel ... you might be the chosen messenger... and maybe through grace you might be given the gift of finding out ... that you were the gift bearer a year ago ... in a grocery store ... you might find out ... that you are ... someone's favorite customer.

Being the Hero

The low tire pressure gauge was blinking on the screen in my vehicle. I could feel that uneasy feeling creeping into my chest. What the heck! Not even halfway to my destination on I-94! Is there something really wrong with a tire or is it just a tire a pound or two low? The screen does not tell me which tire and how low it might be.

Mentally I started figuring out how far it was to the next truck stop along the freeway. I knew it was at least five miles and it was COLD outside.

The wind was whipping around this small out-in-the-middle-of-nowhere truck stop as I pulled in, on this November Minnesota morning.

In the cramped truck stop parking area, I called my husband, and we began discussing the situation. As we talked, I watched a trucker with a beard climb up into his 18-wheeler and he was parked right next to the air hose!!!! I excitedly thought, "This is my chance! I'm sure he will check my tires for me."

I quickly got off the phone and hustled over to the driver sitting up high in the truck. Looking up at him in the truck

I explained the low tire pressure gauge was ON in my vehicle and asked for help putting air in my tires. He looked over at my vehicle and he said, "The tires look fine."

I explained again, "But, I've got a low tire pressure warning flashing on the screen in my vehicle ..."

He said in a placating tone, "Well, do you have a tire gauge in your car?"

Sheepishly I said "No"

He said matter-of-factly, "Well, most places don't have a tire gauge ... they just give you the air. The tires look fine" he said dismissively, as I looked up at him sitting in his truck. I said, "OK thanks!" and turned around to walk away. As I strode away, he said indifferently, "Good luck."

I decided to go inside the truck stop. There were three men in various locations of the store. One was choosing food from the premade sandwiches case ... another man that was shopping in the junk food aisle ... then the third broad-shouldered burly kind of guy was in front of me at the checkout counter. I was certain one of these three would help me put some air in my tires.

The woman behind the first checkout counter was taking money from the broad-shouldered burly customer for his purchases. Another female employee at the second checkout window asked if she could help me. In a cramped tiny convenience store like this, I knew that *everyone* in the store would be able to hear me.

I said, "Well, I need some help checking the air pressure in my tires."

There was a moment of silence. You know what I'm talking about ... that long breath-hold when everyone is waiting for someone else to volunteer... when time seems to hang in the air for a longer than comfortable moment ... I was expecting one of the guys to offer assistance.

Like a lightning bolt of energy, the woman at the first checkout counter said boldy, almost excitedly, "I'll do that!"

With a quick one - handed motion she grabbed her coat and threw it on. It was like watching Wonder Woman swirl into her hero garb! She had a tire gauge in hand as we bolted out of the small building, leaving behind the observers.

The 18-wheeler was gone and the space next to the air hose was unoccupied.

I moved my vehicle to the air hose and together we checked the sticker inside the car door for tire pressure requirements. I didn't have any gloves and neither did she. Wonder Woman knew this was going to be a quick fix. The front passenger tire was 10 lbs. low. She showed me the numbers on the gauge and filled the tire. Then she checked the other tires. They were just a couple pounds low, probably because of the cold.

As she worked, she chatted. Casually she said she has always been a tomboy and loves this stuff ... she said her daughter is a 'girly girl' and loves hair and fingernails and make-up. In an instant, she made me feel at ease ... forgiving myself for not having my own tire gauge ... comfortable with letting her do what she does well.

With the wind biting a bit, she put the air hose back in place. I was waiting to give her a hug. She looked shocked when I pressed cash in her hand. I thanked her profusely ... for stepping forward ... for being willing to help ... for taking five minutes ... for making me feel good.

 Her name was Evonne ... and I am ever grateful I met her.

Sometimes it only takes five minutes to be a PART of life. The guys at the truck stop were non-PART-icipants that day.

Evonne? Yep, she definitely got it! She is willing to PART-icipate in life. She got to be the hero – and being the hero **one day** begets being the **hero another day** – because you get THAT FEELING!   Yes, that feeling inside of being a part of something bigger than just you.

Those guys who turned away when they knew full well that someone right next to them on the planet needed help ... they have no idea what they passed up. They gave away an opportunity to be a hero ... something that was going to make them feel way better than a beer in an easy chair at the end of the day ... I was offering them a gift by asking for five minutes of their time ... but they didn't recognize it as a gift ... Wonder Woman saw the gift ... swirled into her cape ... and without missing a beat ... left everybody else in the dust.

Alone By Myself

10-7-06

My dad, George Ruhland, had been dead five years when I saw the sign. He couldn't have had anything to do with the outcome of what happened that day ... or did he?

I was alone by myself.

I know that sounds strange, but I was on my way to Mankato, MN, going to a Women & Spirituality Conference for the very first time. I felt alone by myself, because I didn't know one other soul that I could talk to about the books I was reading and how my spirituality was changing. Now I was going to a conference that was beckoning me to come.

I 'accidentally' discovered this spirituality conference on that new thing called 'the internet'. I was certain there was no one else near me that was thinking like I was - deviating from the spiritual norm. I was reading books about things like energy and consciousness; things like angels and loved ones watching over us. It was just too far out to think that anyone I knew, would be interested in all this crazy stuff. So, I was going out of town to a spirituality conference ... alone by myself.

I was driving, alone by myself, out in the middle of nowhere, at 60 miles per hour ... with corn fields and sunshine all around. From the top of a small hill, I could see a car across the landscape, and noticed it approaching our mutual upcoming intersection at a high speed. I had the right of way, but I started slowing down.

This country scene was not new to me. The sun was shining, and the feeling of freedom was floating in the air ... I know this feeling, because I was pulled over for speeding on a day just like this (no I did not get a ticket) ... the windows down ... the music blaring ... and it just feels so good ... it was a John Denver singing Rocky Mountain High in the background kind of day. It feels like no one else is on the road and the world belongs to you alone.

By the time he blew his stop sign, I was almost at a complete stop as he entered the intersection. He saw me for the first time as he was making a nearly out of control left hand turn in front of me onto the road. Now he and I both came to a complete stop.

We were side by side, nearly face to face. Because of the corn field, he had no idea I was there. And here we were, so close, it was as if we had planned to just stop, roll down the windows and have a nice country conversation. Compared to my SUV, his car was the size of a pop can. He looked stunned and pale with panic in his eyes. He knew that he had nearly died. I sat there grateful to have it be an incident and not an accident.

The two of us sat there in the middle of nowhere ... in the sun ... alive ... I glanced off to my right. There on the side of the road was a large sign ... not as big as a billboard ... but a sign BIG enough that no one would miss it ... in capital letters it said RUHLAND.

That's all ... just RUHLAND.

The sign took my breath away ... I stared at it ... just sitting there in my car. I paid no attention as the other car drove away. RUHLAND all in capital letters ... I was shocked ... "Dad!" I thought "Were YOU watching me? What are you doing here? Dad! Did you see that other driver, even before I did?"

Now it was my turn to sit in my car stunned and dazed ... What does this mean? This quirk, this fluke, this happenstance. The rest of my trip to Mankato was uneventful and filled with thoughts of dad and the bond between us.

At the conference, I took classes that opened my mind to the coincidences and connection between physical humans and the unseen realm of angels and loved ones.

Here, with these people it seemed a normal assumption that those on the other side were actively involved and communicating with those left behind.

I was surprised and pleased to see a few people I recognized from Alexandria. One woman from our town was having a cigarette outside and I started a conversation with her – she had been to this conference several times and did not imply that these out of the ordinary concepts were out of the ordinary at all!

As the weekend came to an end, I was ready to get on the road. I wanted to find that sign! I wanted to find out what that sign was really there for? Was it a political campaign or an election of some kind? Was it a commercial sign from a seed company by the corn field? Did the sign say anything else in small letters underneath the name? Who put it there? I was antsy to drive home.

I took the exact same route home. I was on high alert, looking and hunting through every country intersection, trying to find the sign with my dad's name again. I checked and watched all the way home ... intersection after intersection.

I never found the sign ... never a hint of anyone campaigning ... nothing. No name on a mailbox or somebody with the last name of RUHLAND running for a political office. I was looking for some legitimate ... logical ... rational reason to have such a sign there ... someone with that last name ... why would there be a sign ... right there?

As the years have passed since that day, now I know that the sign was there for me. If I were to see that sign today, I would shriek out loud and say "THANKS DAD! I LOVE YOU TOO!"

Now I have read and heard literally thousands of accounts of this communication and connections that are easily more vivid than my story, more compelling and more verifiable than my story. Since that day, now when the veil lifts between dad and I ... I just say thank you.

That day years ago ... driving to the conference I thought I was alone by myself ... now I know ... without a doubt ... I was not.

Foresight
March 14 2022

On the new white snow and traffic was slower than normal, I was driving at about 50 miles an hour when I looked up ahead and saw a good-sized deer, standing **in the road**. I mean intentionally completely stopped … broadside … oh yes, like a crossing guard, imposing as heck! This deer was NOT going to move. Even though I couldn't see another deer, I slowed down.

This strong lady had my complete attention now, as she meandered to the other side. I touched the brakes and even though I was down to 30 miles an hour I started to slide … and two more young deer started across the road.

She had planned.

How did she know the roads were slippery?

How did she know she needed to allow more space and time for her babies to cross?

She had foresight – not fear. There's a big difference. Fear would **have stopped them from crossing the road at all.** Foresight allowed her to **think ahead and plan** … from one mamma to another… I have to say … she's pretty darn smart.

Free Session
2016

His wife had died several times one night at the hospital emergency room. She was recovering ... but he was not.

The man who sat in my office was completely stressed out. Alcohol had become his coping mechanism every evening drinking a six pack of beer and now he wanted me to tell his subconscious mind that he would never drink alcohol again.

Woah! I was NOT going to do that! The subconscious mind could throw him into immediate and sudden withdrawal! A drastic change at the subconscious level can be difficult for the body/ mind to adjust.

Truth be told, I was scared! Just a few years into this hypnotherapy career, I had never been asked for help with alcohol before and I didn't have a clue where to start. It seemed that clients were coming with more complicated issues and sometimes I wondered if I could help with such big problems.

I opted to take the coward's way out; I decided to work with the anxiety and stress level that CAUSED the drinking, hoping the alcohol consumption would disappear as the stress response in the body diminished.

He said his wife's medical situation was gobbling up their money. It was hard for me to ask him to pay for the first session, but I HAD to! Studies show, if someone gets something for free, they tend to not take it seriously. I wanted him to take this seriously and follow through on using the prescribed audio 'homework', to clear his mind of anxiety and stress.

At the same time I was working with a professor who taught at the Univ of MN. She was getting excellent results for her issues - they resolved quickly and easily in just two sessions. As she was leaving my office, she voiced how appalled she was at how **low my rates** were. She paid for her session and donated $100 as a gift to use for someone who needed it.

I knew exactly who this money was meant for.

As I expected, my client with the ill wife, was **doing everything I asked him to do** – he was motivated to get this issue fixed as quickly as possible and was getting brilliant results! As he listened to anxiety release audios every day, he began to feel WAY better and slept well each night. His alcohol consumption was plummeting and this second session, was to clean out any residual stress and anxiety permanently.

While he was coming out of trance, I told him that someone had given me a pay-it-forward gift and his session was free. His eyes got wide with excitement like he had won the lottery!!!

"Oh! Oh!" he said in shocked excitement! He literally had no words ... grateful and appreciative ... he thanked me and hugged me many times before leaving the office. I don't think I've ever seen anyone so thrilled by a small windfall!

I called him a couple months later, just wanting to make sure that his wife was fine and the alcohol issue was gone, and he assured me that it was!

ONE YEAR LATER

In October of 2017 one day I was forced to park in the back lower parking lot at the office. The other parking lots were full and I **never** parked in the back parking lot. It's the busiest part of the building since it's also the driver's license testing station. On this chilly day I pulled into a parking spot, got out of my car, and went around to the passenger side to grab my briefcase and lunch.

I was surprised to hear a male voice behind me say, "Do you remember me?"

I turned and looked at the man's face and I lied, "I do remember you, but where did I meet you?" I asked.

He said to me, "You helped me stop drinking alcohol and it really worked! I haven't had a drink in over a year!" Then I recognized the man and remembered the free session.

He thanked me profusely again, gave me a couple of warm hugs and said it was quite a coincidence that I happened to be getting out of my car at the same time he was in the parking lot. His son just happened to be having his driving exam today. He wanted me to know that even now, he appreciated my help. I hugged him hard, and I thanked him.

I tucked that thoughtful compliment away in my heart. I needed to keep that feedback at the forefront of my mind. In those early years, I doubted and fretted a lot over what to do with every client. I spent hours poring over textbooks and fell into bed each night exhausted, feeling like I could never do enough ... or learn enough ... or be enough.

Now I've become more seasoned and confident. That day back in October of 2017, **I needed that man's words as desperately ... as he had needed me a year earlier.**

I marvel at the magic of the Universe, to orchestrate the money for a man in need ... at the exact time he needed it. That same man came circling back around ... on an unspecified day ... at an unspecified time ... in the back parking lot that I never used ... a full year after his appointments ... to give me something WAY more valuable than money ... he gave me words of encouragement.

Call it karma ... call it angels ... or Divine intervention; call it the Universe in action; it doesn't matter. It's the magnetic pull of **love and kindness ...** coming full circle in the world ... unseen forces that pull one person to another ... at just the time ... when I needed it most.

Welcoming Tatum

The two forlorn, lost, and pitiful parents sat there in a semi darkened hospital room, not saying a word. There was nothing wrong – not really – they had been asked to wait another couple of hours for a blood test before being able to take their brand new second born baby home. The blood test would prolong their stay by a couple of hours and possibly even one more night depending on the results. The tired parents were exhausted and all they wanted was to go home!

One year ago it was the Friday before **Mother's Day** when a first baby was born to them … when Cameron Joseph Weber came into the world.

This year it's the Friday before **Fathers Day** when a baby was born .

I was taking care of Cameron as my son and his wife left for the hospital to give birth to baby girl Tatum. The scheduled C section was at 1:30. That means that the whole family was waiting! Everybody knew what time and what day the new baby would become an official part of our family and everybody wanted to stay in the loop.

ME? I got to be 'command central'! There was a barrage of text messages coming into my phone from family members wanting an update. The person that blew up my phone the MOST was 14-year-old Maggie.

Just two months earlier I spent some time in the Arizona sun with granddaughter Maggie, laughing and giggling and shopping together. We shared the upcoming excitement of a new baby in the family and Maggie could not **wait** for her new baby cousin to arrive! The text message would beep, and ask, "Any news yet?" It was Maggie and I would message her back and say 'No not yet'.

There had been multiple delays getting into surgery. By 4:30 PM uncle Rob's message read, "Should I be worried?"

Finally, late in the day the news arrived that little Tatum was here.

A full mop of dark, soft hair and a petite little face. Her fingers were so long, that the first time I saw her, I wanted to take her down to the front lobby of the hospital where a grand piano sits and tell her to just go ahead and play it now.   She was picture perfect.

I took Cam to the hospital to meet Tatum. I explained to him that mom and dad would be home in a day or two with his new sister and about all the fun they will have together.

Cam had a diaper rash our first morning together; I decided to put him in the bathtub to soak for a while. I took his diaper off and let him crawl naked as I readied the bath. As I turned around, I saw that he was peeing on the carpet. Sigh!

I cleaned that up and put the little guy in the bathtub. A few minutes later he proceeded to poop in the tub. Sigh!

I was finishing cleaning up the tub and saw that once again Cameron was peeing on the carpet. Sigh!

Cam and I played and waited patiently for mom and dad to come home.

For the new mom and dad, the very last day in the hospital was glum to say the least! They had been told to wait for another blood test from the baby before they could go home. I could tell on the phone they were greatly disappointed. Their trip home with the new baby had been postponed awaiting one more test.

But I had a secret weapon that I knew would irradicate the lost and forlorn feelings.

I packed up little Cameron and did **not** tell mommy and daddy that we were heading to the hospital. Cameron, in his stroller, smiled and waved at everyone as we entered the hospital and took the elevator up to the birthing floor ... we quietly opened the door and stepped into their room.

They expected a nurse or an aide to come through that door and in a moment they saw their little Cameron had come to play! There was a ROAR of DELIGHT from the two parents that lit up the dark and gloomy room!

And play they did!

Cam climbed on the bed with momma to snuggle. He read books with daddy and climbed all around the room practicing his new found walking skills. Soon two hours had slipped by like a scarf through the hand of a magician. The nurse arrived with the good news that they could go home!!!! Cameron to the rescue!

In short order everyone was home and there was a feeling that all was right with the world.

Later that day, Tom and I took Cam across the street to the park in the stroller, while mom and baby had time to nap. We walked a couple of blocks with the stroller and talked. At the park I went up the slide and Tommy handed little Cam up to me .... Cam and I slid down together for the first time. Tom saw the baby swing that I have taken pictures of Cameron in. On the merry-go-round Tom pushed Cameron and I, grandma and grandson together, for the first time.

The days melded together as Tatum settled into being home. Momma doing the nursing and daddy doing the rest and Cameron getting used to a new baby in the house.

At one point I was searching for Tom and Cameron and couldn't find them. I looked outside; the garage door was up, the stroller was gone, and I walked to the corner of the block; looked down the street and saw my son with his son, strolling together ... the two of them ... a quiet moment. I saw it ... I captured it ... I loved it.

Why am I writing about all of these small, tiny things? The first time with Cameron on a slide and a merry-go-round? Seeing my son with his son strolling together ... why did I put this in a document years ago and let it sit there in my computer and in my mind?

Because the tiny things flow together ... sometimes we forget that the tiny little moments make up the monumental days and weeks and months of our lives. When I say that my heart is overflowing with tiny keepsake moments, I really mean it.

Before I left their house yesterday, to go back to my home, Tommy and I cried together.

I cannot describe ... nor can I explain ... what it has meant to me to be an intimate part of this time in their life. I was just staying out of the way and helping out. It may seem like just a mother-in-law going to help for a few days ... but it's way more than that ... it is a new, tender and fresh life that has been flawlessly and seamlessly added to the EARTH ... and we pretend it is all normal ... but it is miracle stuff ... it is star stuff from God. And they let me in on it ... OMG ... REALLY Oh-My-God! They let me share the miracle.

When the week was over, and I drove an hour and half home ... the message I sent to my son was ... "an hour and a half drive home ... was not long enough ... to count my blessings."

"I Can Take Him Anywhere."

"We can look at the tractor" I said to Joe " if we can stop at the garage sale across the road afterwards. Deal?" "Done!" he said.

It was a casual Saturday. Joe and I were going to the lake to play for a while with grandchildren. Along the old country road Joe saw a tractor that he wanted to look at. I turned around in the next driveway approach and saw a garage sale sign posted there. So, I had bargained with Joe.

My dad had an antique business that was outfitted completely through garage sales. The truth is, I have my dad's curiosity ... I'm just plain curious about what I'm going to find. It's the hunt. Everybody in my family knows about my habit of wandering into garage sales. My daughter-in-law has stopped asking me where my newest summer dress came from, because she knows it either came from a garage sale or a thrift store.

I stayed in the car as Joe looked at the tractor and then we meandered down the road to the garage sale.

An elderly couple in their eighties sat in the garage. When we stepped into the garage these two people were just sitting, not speaking, both of them were looking off into the distance.

She was sitting on a tall stool next to the card table 'check out' area near the door into the house. I was looking at various kitchen gadgets and I could hear Joe talking with the gentleman. I overheard that this couple had been married for 65 years. Joe had immediately engaged her husband in conversation as he sat in a lawn chair about 10 feet away

As I browsed, I heard Joe and the man talking about tools and antiques and I thought to myself "this conversation could take a very long time." Joe can carry on a conversation with anyone. It made me think of a statement my mom used to make, when one of kids were too young and immature to carry on an adult conversation – on the way home she would say, "I **can't** take you anywhere". I had in some way embarrassed my mother with my behavior or lack of maturity.

Joe and I were the only shoppers there and I commented to the woman about a intricately carved wooden box - I had no use for it, but I commented to her something about how original and beautiful it was.

As I approached the woman to pay for an item I said, "You're cleaning some things out I see!"

"Yes" she said, "I'm dying of cancer".

I focused on her, our eyes met and referring to the cancer, I softly asked, "Are you ready?"

I could feel myself settling in for a conversation. One of those dialogues when you know that you are in a particular place ... at a particular time ...for a particular reason. She voiced her concerns and worries about her husband being alone ... no one there to take care of him ... and how will he live without her. She and I talked for 15 or 20 minutes until another shopper arrived.

All the while Joe was engaged in conversation with her husband.

Joe had been looking at a duffle bag but decided not to buy it. As we were leaving, the old man picked up the duffle bag and gave it to Joe. An offering for his kindness ... Joe's gift of listening ... or maybe his gift of taking a few minutes to distract the man from his unending stream of thoughts. Whatever it meant to the husband, it was important enough to give Joe a gift.

As the two of us walked arm in arm back to the car. I quietly said to Joe, "She's dying." and he replied, "I know". The men too had been discussing the impending loss.

We got in the car and I started backing out of the driveway. I said to Joe "You are so amazing! **I can take you anywhere.** Most people put up walls around the subject of dying, and you just take it as it comes. You can handle a chain saw ... you can handle a tractor ... and just as adeptly and lovingly you handle a conversation with a man whose wife will soon depart. I don't' even have words for how much I admire you. **I can take you anywhere.**"

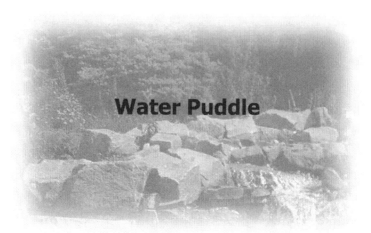
Water Puddle

The dark blue clouds, heavy with rain lined the horizon behind the lake. The surface of the water is a reflection that allows you to see the rain from a "different perspective. " Watching a rain cloud approaching is vastly different on land as opposed to on water. There are no fields or roads or trees or fences, nothing but the surface of the water.

On the other side of the lake, the cloud opened up and was moving our way. I had never experienced before watching the surface of the lake, experience the downpour, and the beating of the rain cloud opening up, creating a definitive line that was moving our way. One side of the line, the chaos of water droplets beating the surface of the lake. The rain hitting the surface created a curtain of chaos that wouldn't let us see beyond its line.

On our side of the line the lake surface was calm yet, but the cloud was coming. We all stood inside the cabin watching mother nature and the show going on before us … the line of chaos coming closer to the cabin until the rain was downpouring on the roof above with sheets of water flowing down the windows. We were all gawking.

There was almost a reverence in the cabin that hushed the adults and children as the sound of water on the roof stole the show. Mother nature, wow! You win!!

As the rain cloud moved on to do its work, it moved past our little spot in the world. The droplets slowed and the intensity of the wind softened and with a sparkle in his eyes, my son said, indirectly inviting his children to play in the puddles, "I wonder who is going to go out in the rain to bring those last toys in?"

The smile on his face had three toddlers in a tizzy of excitement! Five-year-old Cam immediately stepped into the rain going to the deepest pooled water. Then four-year-old Tatum followed outside, and eventually two-year-old Taylor cautiously entered the rain.

They were in and out with wet feet and towels and mom and dad saying, "stay on the towel when you come in ". All the things that parents and kids say back-and-forth as they grow and play and learn.

The water had puddled deeper on one end of the cement ... sudsy from bubble solution being spilled less than an hour earlier. Mother Nature was cleaning up our mess and just like that, the sidewalk chalk drawings, and the bubble solution were gone, creating a new canvas, a new background to begin again, later today or tomorrow or the tomorrow after tomorrow.

As I watched the shenanigans ... a memory was being excavated inside my mind. It was gurgling up there as if it were coming up from someplace deep inside.

I had forgotten that there was a downpour like this when my three sons and I were growing up together decades ago. Those days that I thought were the hardest times and somehow they have now become the best part of my life. That time when I had to stand on my own two feet and lead three young boys into their future.

Way back then, I'm sure we stood at the windows gawking just like we had tonight at a cloudburst. When the downpour subsided, all those years ago, I KNEW where I was taking my sons.

"Get your swim trunks on!" I nearly shouted to my boys. "Get your swim trunks on!" I hollered again. In wide eyed disbelief, sort of like today, they scampered in disbelief up the steps to their rooms coming down with swim trunks on.

With everybody loaded up in the van, we drove just a few blocks to the American Legion Park – a low-lying outdoor basketball court ... right now it was the BIGGEST MOST GIGANTIC WATER PUDDLE in town! On my young boys the water was waist deep ...

One time earlier in the summer it looked like a lake after a heavy rain. I remembered thinking to myself, the next time this happens, I'm taking the boys swimming. Now I had my chance.

I took them to play in the water that had flooded the basketball court. We were the only ones there in the brilliant sunshine that followed the rain. I was thrilled that we were the only ones there. We were the only ones thinking outside the box saying, "Hey! Let's go swimming in the gigantic puddle!"

In real time now I watched the cloud work its magic dancing with the lake, and the children dancing with joy in the puddles outside. I asked my son, "Do you remember the time ... as my voice trailed off and even before the question was out of my mouth ... our eyes were locked and he was slowly nodding his head with a sparkle in his eyes ... a smile on his face ... and in that instant we were sharing that private unspoken experience of the giant water puddle from days long gone by.

I wonder if his extra-long hug that night ... a hug that was tighter and closer than usual ... was the awareness of a gift so magnificent ... that it is beyond putting into words. The two of us together ... watching **his** children splash and at the same time ... sharing a private memory from decades ago ... just between the two of us ... all at once. What a gift!

Gifts of the Heart

A flurry of unexpected gifts have been coming into my life. To the point where I've been questioning what's going on?

One day a couple of weeks ago a girlfriend called me and said that she wanted to talk to me at my office. I had a break in the day at 2:00 PM, so she stopped by. She had wrapped packages – one under her arm and several more in her other hand. She had copied and printed photos of our newborn grandchild that had been posted on Facebook and had started a photo album for me!!! She also framed three of the pictures in five by seven frames! I was stunned! What an incredibly thoughtful and heartfelt gift.

 She died just a few months ago now – she had stopped me in the bank parking lot to say that she was dying ... that afternoon I brought her a bushel basket Fall arrangement ...

On Friday I got a call from my niece Cindy saying that she was building a new house and was moving in a month or so. She has been cleaning out her books and giving things away to Good Will. Of the multitude of books she owned she kept only three. One was the Bible one was Jesus Calling and the third one was the Beach I Walk On. She said I want to read whatever else you've written! I was so stunned by the telephone call and touched to my very core.

One of the most touching gift of words I have received was from Greg, a friend of ours. When Greg finished reading my books he said to me, " Now I know why Joe fell in love with you".

 I was presenting at a meeting one night and HAD to do just one more errand before I went to the meeting. I stopped at the library to pick up a book. Because I was presenting at the meeting that night I was in a dress and tights and high heals. There was a truck parked at the entrance to the main doors to the library in a drop off and pick up area with plenty of room for another motorist to go around if necessary. There was a man in a truck sitting there with windows down just waiting for someone. I said hello to him through the open window and he nodded. I could feel him watching me. You know what I mean, everybody knows that feeling.

Leaving the library, after retrieving my book, the same truck was still there. Walking past the open window and the man said quietly and sincerely, "You ARE beautiful."

It was not threatening or tactless in any way. I smiled a 'thank you' and beamed all the way to my meeting. What a gift!

A high school friend, Weez, after reading my first book wrote : "Your book did not disappoint. In fact, I read it all in one sitting. Once again, I could sense your genuinely sweet spirit. I cannot imagine how grateful your daycare families were to have you care for their kids. Children are great judges of character, so most certainly they loved being around you. And when you talk about experiences with your now-adult sons my heart melts and the tears flow. It's just so lovely to see how you love your boys and how much they love you. If there's ever another book on the horizon, please put my name at the top of the "I want that book" list. I can't get enough of your stories. Thanks again for having the foresight to keep track of the precious experiences and then sharing them with others. It was pure enjoyment for me to read! Don't stop now!"

Just putting these entries together here makes me **squirm** ... it feels uncomfortable and yet fabulous ... at the same time. I'm sure I was taught my entire life to be modest by my parents, and to not brag – and yet at the same time, I realize that these people are telling me – in real time – how I have helped them on their journey through life. They are giving me valuable feedback ... in a positive way.

Why is it so easy for us accept criticism – or to be self-critical; saying to ourselves "**Yup, that's me.** I need to work on that! "

Marianne Williamson wrote "Our deepest fear is not that we are inadequate. Our deepest fear is that we are powerful beyond measure. It is our light, not our darkness, that most frightens us. We ask ourselves, Who am I to be brilliant, gorgeous, talented, fabulous? Actually, who are you *not* to be? You are a child of God. Your playing small doesn't serve the world."

So I am celebrating me and leaving this document in my third book …even though it makes me cringe. And I hope & hope & hope, that I grow to love myself enough, that at some point in the future I can read it and say, **'Yup that's me!"**

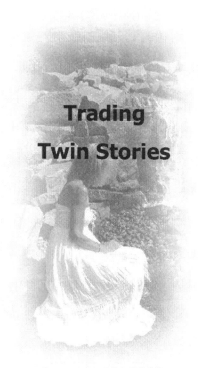

Trading Twin Stories

January 19, 2020

Sunday morning is telephone 'twin time'. I wait for Carol to text or call whenever it fits.

This particular Sunday morning, I was telling Carol about my time in Arizona with my grandson Brady. As my story unfolded I could tell Carol had a story of her own to tell...

Brady and I had been talking for hours that day. When I say hours, I'm **not** joking. This had been our time to talk endlessly. Light conversation and deep conversation. I told him about things he had never heard before. Things about his dad, my son, and events that formed and shaped him in his growing up years.

Brady was totally engrossed in the narrative ... and so was I. Parents never think to tell their kids about their lives. It's not because there's anything to hide, it just that it usually doesn't come up. We assume that our children know everything about us, but, they know nothing about us, nothing about the past that actually formed our perspective.

When Brady and I are alone we are magical ... just all the time in the world ... nobody wanting anything from either one of us ... the occasional interruption of a dog floating in and out was the biggest responsibility we had!

With the wine that evening, Brady was well aware that I was fading fast, and it was time for me to sleep. I got up to leave. My bedroom was just around the corner. All I had to do was walk to the casita. It was no big deal. The Casita is inside a fenced yard, so there was certainly a feeling of safety all around me.

As I got up to leave, my 22-year-old grandson with the injured knee, hobbled beside me ... his hand around my waist ... directing me around a water hose that was laying on the sidewalk ... every step of the way ... he is injured, and I am fine ... but still **he is making sure** that I get safely to my bedroom.

(I know that the first time Brady reads this story, he is going to be saying in his mind, "Of course I make sure my grandma gets to her room OK!")

As he opened the door to the casita for me, he reminded me to pull the drapes ... he hugged me ... told me he loved me ... and I know for sure that he was standing outside my door waiting to hear me throw the deadbolt. As I closed the door behind me, I shook my head and felt his love filling me as I stood there in the safety of my bedroom.

As I finished telling my story, I could hear Carol's tears as I finished telling her about Brady walking me to my bedroom.

Now it was Carol 's turn to tell me a story.

Tim, her son, had invited her to come over to visit at his apartment. While she was there, she laid down to take a nap. That surprised me!

I said "What? You go to someone's house to visit and you take a nap?"

I thought 'who does that?' When I questioned her about it, she said she naps almost every time she goes over there.

"Seriously?" I asked.

I could never take a nap at a time like that – my fear of missing out would not allow it.

When she woke up from her nap, Tim and his girlfriend were at the table talking in the kitchen. Carol joined them and the three of them went on to talk for another hour and a half ... that quiet easy flow of conversation as the weather outside took care of itself.

At 10:30 PM it was time to say goodbye and goodnight as she hugged her son not once ... but twice ... and then came back for a third hug, in a way that a young son tolerates ... and an older son welcomes.

The weather of winter had continued unfolding without permission as she prepared to leave the warmth of the cozy apartment. They had been, just like me and Brady, just letting the world go on all around ... paying attention to only the small private world of conversation ... the closeness that settles into your bones when the conversation melds hearts together. Without noticing the ice storm outside, the warmth of conversation made it so easy to ignore when there is nowhere to rush off to.

Tim put his coat on and walked Carol to her car. He held her arm ... watched and walked her safely to her vehicle ... made sure that the ice was clearing from the windshield ... and asked for a text message after she got safely inside the house.

Carol and I both know that love is the never ending gift ... the one that takes your breath away ... when a son walks you to your car ... in the ice and snow and a grandson walks you to your bedroom in the heat of the desert.

Both Carol and I know we have been gifted this time and this place together ... to be on this planet ... with love flowing so deep ... that we speak it with the tears of a mother ... and a grandmother ... each with a story to tell ... a story so profoundly small ... that one would argue it could never be a topic of conversation ... and yet the two of us tumble out every detail ... every part ... from one to the other, as if it needs to be chronicled for history.

And when the telling is over and the tears are beginning to dry ... we sit in the silence ... two meaningful memories ... two moments so rich ... that they become a part of each other ... twins – that is what we are ... I will hold her story forever ... and she will hold mine.

God In My Office

I walked out of my office in a daze.

Just two hours earlier, shortly before my client had arrived, I looked up to the corner of my room where the 'little children angels' appear to me.

Yes, that's right, a whole row of angels, mostly little angels in training. They have been with me since I first rented this office.

Years ago, I remember searching for office space. It was like going to check out a school before your first day of kindergarten. Self-doubt filled me. Can I really do this hypnosis thing? I was scared.

The building manager left me alone to get a 'feel' for the space. She encouraged me to feel the energy of the room. What? I didn't know that the building manger and I would speak the same language. I sat down on the floor in the corner and asked the room if it was Okay for me to be working there ... to help people, using this new thing I had learned. This thing called hypnosis.

Looking up toward the corner where the ceiling meets the wall, I saw a long row of little child-angels begin to appear. Leading at the very front of the row was a much larger angel and they were all applauding . I knew I was being welcomed to this office space.

It became my routine each time I entered the office to look up and be welcomed by them.

Yesterday before I started the session I looked up to that particular corner and asked the children-angels, the happy beautiful little spirits, to be with me and as always, they appeared there and agreed.

The session began as any other session, with a relaxing induction and my prepared-ahead-of-time script. As I got about a third of the way through my prepared material, I was aware that I was beginning to speak not for myself. That the words were not mine. It felt like there was a love energy or a God energy that was speaking through me.

With my eyes closed I sensed in my mind's eye that there was a bright yellow gold tube of light coming into the top of my head, going down into the trunk of my body to my heart. At my heart, the light took an abrupt turn toward my client as if it were a plumbing elbow pipe under a sink, moving the light directly into my client.

Words that were not mine, tumbled out. I was speaking the words, while at the same time feeling the great love that was flowing to her ... through me ... but not from me. While these messages were being delivered to my client, there were tears streaming down her cheeks and mine too.

God told her that her journey was very simple now and told her to be watchful for signs in her life - that there is a mission for her and part of the information that she needs for her mission will also come through future hypnosis sessions.

She was told that in her daily work of answering 911 calls, she was being heard. Each time an emergency call came to her desk , she looked up, prayed silently, and invited God to help those in dire need. (I did not know any of this ahead of time)

I was awestruck when the session was over. I said to her, "It was an honor to be in your presence." I tried to be very aware of the feel of the energy in the room as I sat there. Now instead of a water pipe influx of energy there was a sense of energy dissipating at a slow rate moving toward the window.   We sat looking at one another. There was nothing to say. When we finally did speak, she verified that every time a 911 call came into the office, she looked up and asked for help.

Maybe I knew ... or was hoping this was just the beginning.

As time went by I created a ritual opening the office each day – checking with the group of angels each time... messages from my BIG angel began to come more directly and the little angels slowly began to disappear one at a time ... they knew I didn't need them anymore ... I was trusting now, knowing that Guidance was there.

The big angel up in the corner still hangs around and checks in once in a while ... but the little ones are all gone. They were helping me in my infancy. There was no doubt about WHY they were there - they were cheering me on - I am certain they were holding my hand and keeping me composed.

One time when I was nervous, a little angel appeared in front of me during a session giving me the thumbs up! I almost laughed out loud!

I don't know when the little angels left. Maybe as I became more self-confident I didn't call on them so much. Maybe when I started inviting my clients' angels to come to the office and help, maybe they knew I was on the right track. I don't know.

It was as if ... when my novice-self could toddle around a bit ... and trust my angels ... and trust my clients' angels ... then the little angels job was done.

Maybe I needed them to look small the way they did — for my benefit ... because I sure felt small.

Maybe I needed them to make me smile and relax through the doubt ... worry ... and fear of my infancy.

Maybe they held my hand more than I knew ... bolstered my confidence ... preparing the way ... for THAT day ... for God in my office.

Maybe ... just maybe ... the little children angels ... came to see God that day too.

The Rocking Chair

"Stop by anytime! You are welcome any time!" That is what they had said. So we took them up on the offer.

One weekend each year, descendants of grandma and grandpa, Mike and Kate Ruhland, make themselves at home in the tiny town of Morton, MN. Morton is where our childhood memories began and still remain. It was at the Morton casino at our annual cousin's reunion, a few years earlier, that we ran into the couple who now own grandma and grandpa's farm . And this was when they had said to us; "Come over anytime!" and we knew they meant it.

We were all just kids when grandma & grandpa were alive, so this group that wanted to stroll down memory lane, had a hard time remembering the old gravel roads that weave between corn fields to get to the farm. With two carloads of cousins ready to go, our Uncle Jim volunteered that day, to sit in the lead car doing the navigating.

We slowly entered the driveway, looking and remembering. The old weeping willow tree next to the driveway was gone now. The weeping part of the tree, used to hang so low over the driveway that a car's windshield parted the branches and leaves.

As we pulled into the yard, the man who had told us we could stop by anytime, got off his lawn mower and without a moment's hesitation, welcomed all of us. He excused himself for just a second to tell his wife, in the house, that the Ruhland's were here to visit.

We began with a tour of the barn as if it were a mansion with a guide showing us around. "Follow me please ... and now we are looking up at the loft area where the bales of hay were stored. " The inside walls of the barn still have the metal Certified Seed signs hanging. As a small girl, the barn seemed a LONG way from the house - now, as an adult, it was much closer.

As we explored the property, I realized, this was my first time leaving the main yard. I walked in places I was not allowed to go as a child. The lush green grass flowed lazily down to the creek - the water just meandering along. A fallen tree on the side of the creek was laying on the ground with roots still hanging over the water. It would have acted as a magnet if we were all still children. Right now, I wish I had not listened all those years ago - because I saw a paradise I had no idea existed!

My cousin Tom asked, "Haven't you *ever* been back here before?" "No" I said "I was told not to leave the yard."

The grin on his face said that he too had been told, only he was the smart one, he had not listened.

When I was a little girl, there were rows of apple trees from the house to the gravel road. Now one lone apple tree remains from what was once our grandma and grandpas 'orchard'.

We rambled on the property well over an hour and by the time we finally entered the house, there was warm bread sliced on a platter - the coffee was hot and the table set and ready for us as if we were visiting royalty. All the while, our hosts encouraged us to talk and tell them the history of this land that is now in their keeping.

As I entered the living room the memories were coming back to full size in my mind. I gazed at the corner where grandpa used to sit with his pipe in hand, in a rocking chair that was a gift to them on their wedding day.

After intruding on our hosts' afternoon for nearly two hours, we were finally making our way to the door with hugs and handshakes all around, when the lady of the house exclaimed, "Oh but WAIT! I have raspberry jam to send home with each of you!" and of course, the raspberries had been harvested from the front yard. My grandma and grandpa would have wept had they seen the warm country welcome we received from the kindred souls that now care for the land that was once theirs.

The only video that was running that day was the one in our minds. Everyone had their own experiences and recollections flooding through their thoughts. For me, the video that played over and over was the rocking chair ... the wedding-gift rocking chair with one of the back boards broken. Someone had repaired it with a piece of wire, wrapping the wire around and around and around to hold it together. I remembered the day my dad was about to take that chair to the dump and discard it. The varnish was nearly black with over 50 years of dirt embedded in it. I volunteered to save the rocker. It came home with me and I found someone to "dip it" and refinish the over half-century old chair. The black was gone and the oak reappeared. The grin on my dad's face when he saw the refurbished chair was worth all the gold in the world to me.

All three of my sons were rocked in that chair in the warmest, coziest place in our home. Then, a grandson was rocked there and a granddaughter too. Now, in May 2017, another great-great-grandchild of grandma and grandpa's will be born and rocked in that chair.

Grandma arrived in the United States from Germany at the age of 6 with her parents.

But grandpa ... grandpa left Germany ... left his family ... left everything he knew... all by himself ... at the age of 17 ... to create a new life *for all of us ... What kind of guts and courage did it take to step onto that boat ? ... knowing he would NEVER be able to 'go home' again ... never be able to stand on the soil of his birth again ... as we had done that day.*

My thoughts ripple backward through space and time ... honoring those two hardworking and selfless people ... bestowing upon them ... my deep love and gratitude.

This Christmas ... wishing you ... profound gifts of the heart.

    Love, Cathy & Joe

GRANDDAUGHTERS

Friday, July 22 2022

My granddaughter met my granddaughter today.

My blue eyed, blond haired, 18-year-old Maggie, with the happy sassy personality, got to hold her eight-WEEK-old cousin for the first time today.

Seems crazy to have 18 years between granddaughters. Little Lexi will have physical characteristics that are different from Maggie's. She will most likely have dark eyes, brown hair and a deeper skin color as she grows up and into herself.

Little Baby Lexi doesn't know about cousins or anything about growing up yet. She is a snuggling baby girl with nothing but eating and sleeping on her agenda. She doesn't know yet that I am the watcher, the grandma, the keeper of the love. That's right, she doesn't know that the beautiful blond cousin that holds her has been under my watchful eyes for 18 years now – she doesn't know that I am here now to watch her grow.

Yes, my granddaughter met my granddaughter today – a full grown one … meeting a tiny baby … Little Miss Lexi has double the trouble now … Maggie and I both have our eyes on her … both of us adult women now … watching out for our little peanut, Lexi!

THE OAK CHEST

The Amish woman wore a dark blue dress with a tightly closed neckline and skirt that hung down to her ankles. Her hard-working posture seemed to imply that we were interrupting the flow of her day, as the three women in our group stepped onto the rough wood porch. Playing safely near the house was a barefoot little girl in the same blue fabric from neck to ankles. There was a hitching post there for horses, even though there were no horses in sight.

On the front porch of the store, my girlfriends were asking the woman about the impressive massive onions she had grown and the price. But I headed right inside of the wood-working shop. Yes, I had been there before ... had seen her before ... had met her before, but she didn't remember me. Why would she? The last time I was there I told her I would be back to buy at a later time ... she had no idea I really meant it. We were just another vehicle pulling into her driveway, she was obliged to answer our questions and wait ... and so she did.

Inside the Amish wood-working store sat an oak chest with a precisely carved swan on the lid. I immediately went to it - and when I opened the lid there was a contradiction of the senses, because out came the smell of cedar. I ran my hand across the impeccable finish and breathed in the scent. I had looked at a similar one two years earlier before Tom and Brittany's wedding. I wanted to buy one for them then, but the newlyweds had assured me, that the two of them needed nothing. So I only admired it two years ago and tucked the thought away in my mind, promising myself that when the time was right, I would be back.

After inspecting the chest, I walked away to look at vegetables , every so often glancing back at the chest out of the corner of my eye. I was checking and double checking the feelings I had each time. Seeing the beauty of it gave me a warm and comfortable feeling of belonging ... and I could imagine it filled with toys or blankets or whatever...and I knew it was right.

The woman whose day we had interrupted, seemed to soften her facial expression as the three of us began to accumulate purchases ... pickles, onions, watermelon and an oak chest.

When the payments were done, I was about to lift one end of the chest along with a girlfriend, when the sturdy Amish woman looked over at me, and shooed me away like a fly. She picked up my end, with my girlfriend on the other end; the two of them loaded the treasure chest into the back of our vehicle.

Once-upon-a-time, a long time ago, this treasure chest was an acorn. It's past has a sense of an earlier time when the trees themselves were a family, as they grew for decades side by side. The trees sheltered and protected one another for years until their growing time was over. Then, later, the hands of an Amish family carefully constructed the trunk of the tree into something timeless and they filled it with their own old-world values of family and strength and sturdiness.

For months now the chest has been sitting on the workbench in my garage, covered by a soft green blanket, waiting to be delivered ... to the new young family. One day soon, we will deliver that chest to Tom and Brittany's home where little Cameron (19 mo.) and Tatum (6 mo.) are just little seedlings themselves.

The chest appears to be new and empty ... but it is not.

The chest is already holding our whole families' love and protection, just as the big trees sheltered the tiny ones decades ago. With arms outstretched, we form that circle of shelter around our two new little acorns ... letting in just the right amount of rain and abundant sun and overflowing love. The chest is full of love in all shapes, sizes, colors and textures.

There is "Big Uncle Robbie" love cushioning the walls of the chest ... and Maggie's "holding- her-little-cousins-for-the-first-time" gentle hugging love ... and there's Grandpa Mike's peaceful calm pillow of love lining the bottom ... and Brady's "cool dude" blanket of cozy love hidden inside ... then there's Uncle Johnny's "toss-the-baby-in-the-air" kind of love filling it with giggles and Auntie Shannon's "Awwww isn't he cute!" tender kind of love ... and

Grandpa Joe's "can't-wait-to-take-them-on-the-four-wheeler" playful kind of love.

And what about me and my grandma kind of love?

I see my grandma love as the glitter glue that filters down into the chest between the hopes and the dreams and everyone else's love - melting ... joining ... bonding ... a glue that mixes together all the colors, shapes and sizes of belonging and love ... keeping our two new acorns safely ... soundly ... peacefully ... and neatly wrapped in our families' colorful arms of love.

Wishing you LOVE: ... that comes in all shapes and sizes ...

    ... that glitters beyond Christmas ...

        ... that bonds hearts together forever.

            Cathy & Joe

"Hammertime"

8 18 2011

He was nearly crippled. Hammer was slowing down substantially. Gone were the days of finding him chasing wildlife in the early morning and you didn't hear him howling at the moon at midnight like he used to when he was a pup.

Hammer was his name and he gracefully agreed to let us use his name as the Wifi password in our home – it still keeps his memory alive for us.

In August 2011 I was getting ready to leave for the day. Hammer was laying in the **back** yard sleeping peacefully. He could still eat regular dry dog food, but this particular day canned dogfood is what I served in the bowl now and put it in the **front** yard. We needed to use canned food because we daily laced it with a drug ... yep buffered aspirin, as the veterinarian had suggested. I left for the morning knowing that eventually he would wake up and wander from the back yard to the front yard for breakfast. You know, continental breakfast is always ready.

Returning home, to my surprise, at 1:15 PM Hammer was still sleeping in the backyard. Food in the front yard, yet untouched. I carried the food through the house and placed it in front of his nose so the smell would wake him up. He woke instantly and ate until he found the hidden pills. Leaving the pills untouched, he proceeded to wander the yard going about the business of his day. I just left the bowl there; once he had discovered the medication, he'd never be back to finish it anyway.

About dinner time I glanced out the window and saw the neighbor's black lab leaving our yard … the medium-sized dog was crouching in guilt … you know what I'm talking about … tail tucked between his legs, head down, eyes and head scanning from left to right … sneaking away down our country driveway … hoping no one saw him.

I went to the back yard to peek at the food bowl. Sure enough … the neighbors' dog had finished all of the food, including the four buffered aspirin meant for the crippled member of our family. I laughed myself silly!!

Hammer had slept until 1:00 in the afternoon – got his breakfast delivered right to his nose - ate his breakfast - had been wandering around on this gorgeous August afternoon in the country – not a care in the world; as he ages with grace. He chose **not** to take the meds and the young lab pup indiscriminately cleaned the bowl without a second thought.

Hammer **used** to be like the lab … running and chasing at every opportunity … nothing **used** to get away from Hammer. That day, Hammer smelled the scent of the pup on his food dish and I highly doubt that he cared.

I laughed out loud about the different ages and stages coexisting here in the country – one speeding along so fast, he had ingested aspirin with an inhale. 'Dumb damn dog' I think to myself. And then there is Hammer, more discriminating now that he's aging ... making a deliberate choice to eat the food and bypass the meds...both dogs ... in their own way ... living their best life.

Hammer has been gone a lot of years now and even though we can't see him, I'm sure Hammer's spirit is still here ... still loving the country ... a younger version ... still playing in the yard. If you're ever in the neighborhood, help us keep Hammer's memory alive and feel free to log-in ... set a spell ... and maybe as you sit in the yard you will feel a cool dry nose, move up under your hand. The feeling of a dog there; wanting to be petted. You might tell yourself that it was just your imagination ... and then you notice the sound of an animal bolting away through the grass ... as your phone beeps ... you are logged in ... with the password 'Hammertime'.

The Lighter

The young man dropped into line ahead of me seamlessly. The gas station had all of the usual convenience items right there at the checkout and this guy casually chose a lighter.

When he stepped up to the counter to pay for the lighter, the young man behind the counter said, "Oh, you're going to love this lighter!!!!" I was surprised at the enthusiasm. "Yes" he continued, " You can replace the flint. See here…" He pointed at the top of the lighter. Now, turning the lighter upside down he said "… and see … see here, on the bottom? You can refill the lighter fluid with butane." Turning the lighter right side up again, he said " This allows you to use it a really long time! They are really great lighters. I really like them!"

As I stood there in line I looked at the customer in front of me and with a HUGE smile I said, " I don't even **need** a lighter and I really want to buy one of those!"

Now the customer in front of me agreed with a laugh! Pretty soon everybody in line was getting into the act. He laughed and as I turned, the customer behind me was laughing and said, "Hey let's **all** buy lighters today!"

Every one of us stepped out of that convenience store with a smile on our face.

What did it cost? Five people laughing together ... one of those people could have been having a crummy day ... until now. It doesn't take much to put a smile on other people's faces ...it doesn't take much to help people feel connected ... just a willing smile.

You just never know when YOU are the BEST part of someone else's day ... you don't know when you just turned a crummy day into a tolerable day ... and maybe it improved your day too!

   ... talk to strangers ... they need you ... you need them ... everybody can use a smile.

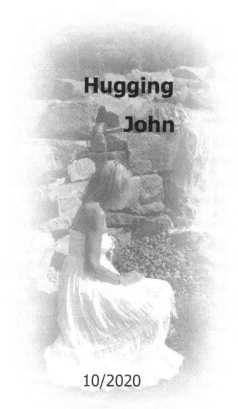

Hugging John

10/2020

I was in Arizona BECAUSE of the pandemic ... I just wanted to be with my son & family and be the mother grounding presence there. That's all, nothing more than to bring the feeling of mom being there.

I was at John's office visiting employees that I have become good friends with through the years; Paula said to me, "I'm so glad you're here. It's so grounding to have your mother near during a time like this."

I was shocked by her comment! It was like she had looked inside my mind and read my thoughts! I said to her "That's exactly why I'm here! I'm just here to sit in the middle of my family for a week and BE here ... nothing more."

During my weeklong visit I kept wishing that we could go back to the way it was before the pandemic. But much of what happened to create my perfect week in Arizona could not have happened if the world was the way it was before. If the world was the way it was before, my 23-year-old grandson probably wouldn't have invited me to come and watch a movie with him in his bedroom, the two of us propped up on pillows and continued our narrative as the two hours rolled by.

Had the world been the way it was before the pandemic I certainly would never have been sitting with Maggie, who was wearing pajamas, in her bedroom with a psychology classroom on a zoom call. She and I were side by side.

6 ½ days of wonderful moments and time together. How am I ever going to tell Joe all of the magical moments that happened?

With or without a pandemic, my solo trips to Arizona always conclude with my alone ride to the airport with my son. The trip to the airport is an exclamation point at the end of the sentence. We don't talk about anything big, nothing monumental really. Just a quiet time together when my thoughts can hold him once again in my arms, like when he was small and when he was all mine.

Then at the airport there's the hug. The last hug at the drop off location on the sidewalk ... just my son and I. I had my purse on my arm while trying to hug him that day. With my face buried in his chest I said to him, "I'm going to put my purse down."

Now it was a full hug, between the two of us ... no words, but lots of communication ... communication that happens beyond what is considered usual or typical. Something had changed ... about what is important and what is not ... and today as we hugged ... he cried too.

We go back a long way John and I.

We know what we had back then – years ago – when he was small and I was young --- carrying him on my hip – but now we both know ... now that he too is a parent of grown up children.

For a long time I was the only one who knew this - now it is different. We have a shared perspective about life ... about how to love ... and about connection. And right now I am filled up with love ... and the overflow is coming out my eyes.

As I boarded the plane, I was grateful for the mask that absorbed the tears flowing down my face. I certainly didn't want to look like I was sick! Not in the middle of a pandemic!

On the other end of my flight, I stepped off the plane and I cried alone as I drove home ... missing John and thinking about what had changed. He understands more now; has a wider perspective watching his own children step into lives of their own. He understands now that I am the woman who has loved him every moment of his life ... as he loves his children every moment of their lives.

I wonder if sometimes he'd like to be small again – for a short time and let me, who loves him every minute, just take care of the world for a little while. Take that responsibility off his shoulders and take a break from life - feeling the freedom ... that neither one of us knew we had ... back then ... when he was small and I was young.

Sometimes I miss John and those long ago times ... in minutes and nanoseconds and heartbeats. How could I not? His heartbeat used to be so close to mine that they were inseparable once upon a time.

 That is why I came to Arizona during a pandemic ... to be THAT woman ... to sit in the middle of my son's family ... and just take care of the world for a little while ... bringing a sense that all will be well ... let me take that responsibility off their shoulders for a while ... and even though I could not kiss away a pandemic   ... still I was there ... to be a steady presence.

I might have said to myself, "Little me? How am I going to be a steadying presence in a global pandemic?" I might have doubted why I was there, were it not for Paula ... Paula in all her wisdom ... was able to see it clearly the very moment I stepped into her office. I needed the validation that tumbled out of her mouth, when she said, "I'm so glad you're here! It's so grounding to have your mother near during a time like this."

Paula knew without a doubt why I was In Arizona ... I had come to tell my son "Go run your company! I'll just move about the house and I will love up my grandchildren and I'll bake them some treats and take their mind off the world right now ... and when I have given my love and a feeling of normality ...   then I'll be on my way home ... and I will collect my favorite hug of all ... at the airport ... hugging my firstborn son, John.

The Lamp

I pulled up to the garage sale and left my purse in the car ... I don't know why, I just knew that I didn't need money.

I started gathering items for Caring and Sharing office - an organization that collects, cleans and distributes to those in need. They deliver whole households of furnishings at one time! I figured I would go get money from the car when I was done shopping.

As I collected items and brought them forward to the table, I told the two elderly comrades I was not buying the items for my personal use. When they found out it was for people in need, THEN they started to load me up with all kinds of items! I did not need any money. They were thrilled to give it to me and to give it to others in hardship! I was pleased to take it to Caring & Sharing!!!! I hauled the items into the office building. Among the items was a floor lamp.

There was something about it that reminded me of the floor lamp in my office. A lamp that I have used for over 40 years. It's been around so long, I don't even notice it much.

This morning lying in bed I was telling my husband about the garage sale and delivering the lamp and other items … and unexpectedly telling him how my lamp came to be with me.

It was a gift from my parents, a brand-new gift, from a furniture store. They let me choose it as a housewarming gift and I suspect they didn't know how desperate our life was at that time. We were destitute. Would they every guess there was a time when there …. was no money …. a time when we didn't have enough food … a time when our house could've been taken away but wasn't because of the generosity of a man who owned the contract for deed.

 It was not pretty.

Years of life went by, with ups and downs, and me emerging on the other side a single and happy mom that was getting my life back together.

I eventually approached the man who owned the contract for deed and asked for the total of back payments that I owed to him. When I paid the back payment and interest in full, he was delighted for **me**! … much more than for himself. I suspect there was a disagreement between him and his wife, she wanting him to foreclose and he refusing. And now he could save face, go home with back payments plus interest, along with a feeling of self-satisfaction that would last forever.

And the same thing happened when I got around to paying off personal loans from my mom and dad. Neither one of them ever expected to see that money returned to them. They didn't care about the money, they cared about my stability. Now they knew that I was going to be just fine. That's what they *really* wanted to know.

Telling the story of the lamp brought back memories from a time when I was at rock bottom ... like the people who turn to Caring & Sharing for help. It is my belief that everyone has a rock bottom in their life. It doesn't need to be financial, it might be emotional, it might be spiritual, it might be physical. It's that time that we measure everything else by ... that one rock bottom time in our life. And we can say to ourselves, "Well this isn't so bad! After all, I survived rock bottom"!

My lamp is from that time of rock bottom ... it came from the two people that allowed me to struggle until I finally got on my feet ... they applauded when I stood up ... I stood solid like the lamp ... and now my light shines.

I hope that whoever got that other floor lamp from Caring & Sharing ... when they were at rock bottom ... I hope they eventually see the benefits that came from that time ... what they learned ... how they grew ... noticing and appreciating who applauded for them when they stood up ... hoping that lamp will shine for them ... like mine does for me.

HUMMER

I am laughing myself silly, watching my five-year-old grandson pushing a Hummer. The bright yellow Baby Hummer was out-of-power, out-of-gas, out-of-charge. Cameron was pushing it across the yard heading for the garage. They have a little Hummer and their Uncle Robbie has a big Hummer ... a REAL one.

The garage holds the power cord for recharging this toy. The garage that stores big people real size vehicles and kid size rechargeable vehicles ... it holds big size lawn chairs and miniature lawn chairs too.

Watching this five-year-old's response to the dilemma, tells me that this situation has happened before. He has learned from someone bigger than himself exactly what to do when the bright yellow baby Hummer has lost power. He pushes from behind, and is bellowing to his sister, "Steer!" " Steer!" Even without power steering he knows that somebody still needs to navigate. Laughter is bursting out of my mouth when the Hummer goes from the sidewalk onto the thick carpet of fertilized grass, with the drag of the grass slowing him down considerably.

Finally, I went over to help him push.

Little sister in the drivers seat was paying no attention at all! For her it was a free ride. I started to help push the Hummer across the grass. When we got to a crucial turning point Cameron said, "Steer!" and Tatum would pay attention for a moment.

When we had successfully veered away from the obstacle in her path, again her attention was drawn to other kids playing. Once again I heard Cam say, "Steer!" and she would veer away from a car or a house.

Then as she was headed for the shrubs in the landscaping Cam said, "Steer!" Time after time came the instructions to "Steer" and we eventually got to the garage.

In the garage the two preschoolers perfectly pulled the hood of the vehicle up and showed me how to disconnect the wires inside. Then they reconnected them to the charging wire which was attached to an outlet on the wall in the garage. They did all this seamlessly ... not running over anyone or anything at all ... and just left the Hummer sitting there ... recharging ....

I enjoyed every minute of pushing the Hummer across the yard next to Cameron as he yipped at his sister, "Steer! Steer!". I loved watching Cameron take charge. He knows when the little yellow Hummer runs out of power, it's something to be solved and it's not a big deal.

He knows that when you are heading toward the corner of the house - change direction. When you're heading toward the street – change direction ... keep an eye on your destination ... and above all ... just like life; STEER!

The Closet

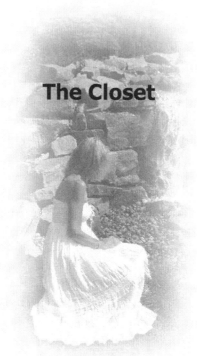

12 9 2020

I didn't tell my son and his wife that I had been in the coat closet that morning.

Having spent the night at Tom and Brittany's house, I was nearly ready to head home, when Brittany asked if I could stay and watch the kids a little while, long enough for her to run an errand. "Of course!" I said.

Cam and Tatum were both done eating breakfast and baby Taylor was still picking at the food on the tray of her highchair. I was about to eat a hardboiled egg with a cup of tea, when I saw 3-year-old Cameron, grinning from ear to ear, open and step into the small coat closet by the door to the garage. My eagle eyes were watching the bifold door for any sign of fingers getting squashed. Soon he was in the closet, all by himself, laughing and giggling, delighted with himself for having found a new place to play while grandma was in charge.

It didn't take long before 2-year-old Little Miss Tatum was in the coat closet right there beside him. Partially closing the door, I watched for little fingers again. The two of them were trampling on top of shoes and boots on the floor of the closet, hooting loudly.

As if the darkness in the closet made him feel like he was miles away, Cameron started to holler at the top of his lungs. "Grandma!!!... Grandma!! ... Wanna come in the closet!?!"

Once again LOUDLY, "Grandma!!!... Grandma!! ... Wanna come in the closet!?!"

With the baby in the highchair contentedly picking away at her breakfast ... Me: the Grandma; the big person; the head honcho; the one in charge for the moment ... I squished myself into the closet, standing on top of shoes and ducking to keep coat hangers from poking into my head and hair. Cam and Tatum were standing underneath the coats, in that cozy open space. There was just enough light coming through the slats in the bifold door, to light the closet with a soft glow.

I kept saying, "watch your fingers, watch your fingers" as Cameron closed the bifold door completely. We stood in the dark giggling and cackling. All of the sudden Cameron burst into song singing, "Twinkle Twinkle little star!!! How I wonder what you are..." at top volume there in the closet. Tatum and I naturally joined the singing of the old familiar tune. When 'Twinkling' wore off, we moved on to Old Macdonald's Farm...

The climax of the cackles wore down, and I told the two of them that we needed to go check on the baby. All of us left the closet, and I thought the shenanigans were over. I sat and ate my hardboiled egg and drank my tea, watching the baby throw food on the floor. 😊

Very soon Cam and Tatum were back in the closet. This time standing quietly in the shadowy light.

"Grandma!! Come in the closet!" "Grandma!! Come in the closet!"

My second invitation into the closet.

This second time in the closet was different. The soft comforting light was coming through the door-folds ... we could hear our breath ... and we just stood there ... silently. Not a sound. I waited for song to break out ... or cackles to erupt ... but nothing ... just deafening silence. As we stood quietly each with our own thoughts ... hearing the beating of our hearts ... without a word ... Tatum put her little hand in mine.

We stood there like that ... side by side ... her small hand in mine, for what seemed like a long time ... until the babbling of the baby in the highchair called us out once again.

Later, as I drove home, I thought about the morning events. I had watched little Cameron get into the closet the first time with excitement and newness and when little Miss Tatum joined him that too was new and exciting. And then when Grandma joined it was different and thrilling ... the second time was peaceful listening to the silence ... but I knew that it was the final time ... the interest in the closet had worn off ...

I did not tell their parents about the experience – what was I going to say? ... we were quiet together in the closet???? It was only on my way home that the magnitude of those few minutes quietly crept deeper into my heart. At the time there were no words ... only feelings ... feelings of quiet love.

Joy surrounded us there in the closet like a toasty warm blanket ... the feel of a soft tiny hand in mine, nearly took my breath away – and do we really fret over what we might give someone wrapped in a box?

It's all so simple ... when hugs and warmth and love is what life is made of ... and isn't that ... what we really want for the rest of our lives? A few ... giggles and laughter ... a small warm hand in ours ... and to stand in the closet ... and be quiet together ...

Wishing you quiet love,

Cathy and Joe

Hunting Rabbit

The scene was unfolding; I was like a newspaper reporter with breaking news!

As we looked out at the frozen lawn you could tell rabbits had been outside eating trees or anything they could find sticking out of the snow.

It all started innocently. You know, a dad and his son and that very first rabbit. There was not an inkling that anything would really come of it; this talk about shooting a rabbit. I mean seriously – how would you shoot a rabbit in the city? on the frozen tundra? in Fargo North Dakota? from a sliding glass door? It's impossible.

Joe and I went home that day and later the real story began, when pictures arrived on our phone. Father and son as a team, one shot the pellet gun and the other one holding the spare pellet, as they shot their very first rabbit.

Texting back and forth would not do! Joe and I got on Facetime to talk to them personally; as if we were news commentators needing to know every single detail. As if we were holding a microphone before them asking which way the rabbit moved or turned and who shot at what time and what time it was when they went outside that very first time to retrieve the rabbit.

Little Cameron stared and stayed back from this first rabbit ... who had died with its eyes wide open, while Tom picked it up and put it in a bucket. I didn't know that others in the neighborhood were trying to limit the number of rabbits as well. One neighbor used snares and still another neighbor came and took the rabbits to make gloves out of the hide. Now I get it; this is a community effort.

****

3 12 2022

And then we come to today - the day before Taylor's second birthday. We are celebrating her birthday, and I notice Tom's eyes scanning the wide open backyard in a sweeping motion, from side to side. It did not cross my mind that he was looking for something in particular. But he was ... he was watching for rabbits. They said that they hadn't seen a rabbit for weeks now, so it never crossed my mind that I might actually get to watch this unfold.

Suddenly Tom started moving fast! Cameron immediately slid off his Uncle Robbie's lap and said quietly, "I'm going to get that damn rabbit."

Father and son in unison – both running to get hunting equipment. They had been waiting and now they were ready.

The sliding door was opened and Tom's 6'4" body easily filling the space as he braced himself inside the doorway, aiming the pellet gun. As he took aim, four-year-old Cameron slid effortlessly between his dad's legs ... Cam bracing himself inside his dad's legs and Tom braced inside the door... I could hardly believe what I was seeing! I stood there gawking at my small grandson taking his place between his dad's braced legs ... not interrupting the shot at all! Just there – exactly where he belongs, right with his dad.

Tom shot the rabbit in the neighbor's yard, and it laid in the snow kicking. Quickly both Tom and Cam got dressed in their winter gear and went outside to retrieve the rabbit so that it wouldn't suffer. Before they walked out the door, I took a quick photo.

Later, when I told Tom that Cam had been between his legs while he was shooting, Tom said "Really?" He hadn't even noticed. I said "Yes! I took a picture!" With a grin on his face he said, "Send me that picture!"

They say that a picture is worth a thousand words ... well that photo captures way more than just a hunting pose. The fact that Cameron was between his father's legs and his father didn't even notice, speaks to the comfort and connection between this big man and his little son ...

There was a time ... a long time ago ... when Tommy and I worked side by side in my daycare. He and I had that same comfort then ... knowing each other so well that we were able to predict each move the other would make.

And there will be a time in the future when Cameron too will have that same comfort with a son or a daughter. It might not be a rabbit that connects them ... but it will be some small, monumental thing that creates a permanent bond ...

And Tom will watch his son ... like I am watching now. I am watching the invisible threads of connection that weave one tiny keepsake moment into a fabric of magnificent beauty. The invisible threads cross over and over and over again ... and somewhere in that mosaic ... hidden in the background ... is a picture of a little boy bracing himself ... inside the legs of his daddy ... and saying, "I'm going to get that damn rabbit!"

Tatum's Hand

March 2 2022 Wednesday.

Six days since little Tatum had the growth on her hand removed. She still won't let anybody take the gauze surgical wrapper off. Her momma has put a plastic bag over it for bath time. The gauze is pretty loose but it seems to give her a sense of safety and comfort. She is self-monitoring her activities while the hand heals.

When my knee was injured, she regularly would ask, "How's your knee grandma?" as we sat on the floor playing with kitchen toys ... somehow, she always knew when I was moving a child away from my knee. My knee is fine now and each child takes their turn sitting on my lap as we play.

Now the tables were turned, and I was watching Tatum protect her hand as we played.

I had a set of air hockey paddles and some pucks that were tucked away from when Brady and Maggie were young. (Oh, who am I kidding? They didn't get saved they just got forgotten! And I came across them at a time when there might a use for them)

I took the kids to the hallway that leads to the bedrooms. They had no idea what to expect as I put the puck on the floor and knocked one of them into the baseboards so that it bounced off, like a sideboard.

They looked at the concept curiously. We kept goofing around with them, Cameron, and I – just gently hitting them back and forth for a while ... casually ... finally after getting a couple of pucks past him out the other side ... then it was as if there was a tumbler that fell into place in Cameron's brain. And he got it! I mean he REALLY got it! He understood I was trying to get the puck past him.

The two of us started a **competition,** batting the puck furiously back and forth, just like when Brady and I used to. Little Cameron at the other end of the hallway was staring me down and laughing the whole time saying, "No you don't! No you don't!" and I said, "Oh yes I do!" as the two of us were laughing wildly!

Tatum tried once or twice ... but holding the paddle and making fast movements with her hand was not going to fit for her today ... she quietly went back to the living room without complaint. Her body was talking to her, and she was listening. Taylor was coming to sit on my lap to watch, but most of the time it was Cameron and I.

That day we decorated Valentine cookies ... painted pictures with watercolor ... made popcorn in an Air Popper ... watched clouds floating by in the sky, by laying on a blanket by the sliding glass doors.

All this before 2:30 naptime.

Their 'naptime delay tactic' was to tell me they wanted me to sing songs and nibble ears before they went to sleep. 'The Wheels on the Bus' was customized for each individual family member. Then comes the quiet kissing time ... nibbling and caressing ... well placed smooches on soft skin. I thanked Cameron for letting me come to play. His soft eyes were relaxing and ready to fall asleep.

I nibbled Tatum's ears, kissed her face, making sure her hand was placed just right on the bed, comfortable for her. I said, "Thank you for playing with me."

"Come back and play again" she said, "and bring Grandpa Joe along."

I walked out of the room with my throat tight and blinking back tears.

"Don't grow up little child ... stay small just a little while longer ... so I can come back to play another day. You can ask me how my knee is ... and I will tell you it's fine ... and I will ask you how your hand is ... and you can tell me it's fine ... and we will sit on the floor once again ... because when there's love sitting in your lap ... we won't even notice if something needs to heal ... love just soaks into that spot ... that place that is healing ... and somehow it heals faster than you ever expected.

Invasion of Privacy
1 2 2023

It is a gorgeous day with high Winter humidity so that every tree is frosty and majestically white. I am driving from Millerville to Alexandria - about 25 minutes. I love County Road 6. It is dry... it is straight... and I am the only one on the road. I can see for miles in all directions – off to the left and the right – in front of me and even behind me in my rear view mirror. I Love this country feeling ... I mean really love it.

I look down and I find my speedometer at 79 miles an hour. I'm listening to music loudly and loving the moment. I am completely safe and in control.

I ponder the thought – wondering when the day is going to arrive that my vehicle in a mechanical voice will speak to me and say, "You are driving 79 miles an hour in a 55 mile an hour zone". In my imagination I look at the console that is speaking to me and I say, "F____ off!"

Conversation Time

3 22 21

"You said you wanted to talk to grandma! So come on over here." Brittany urged little Tatum as I waited with a smile.

Little Tatum brushed her hair out of her face and looked at me on the screen, but didn't know what to say. I asked her how she was and what she was doing. In brief staccato statements she said 'Good' and 'Playing' in quick response to my questions. Soon there was once again awkward silence.

Then Brittany leaned over and whispered to Tatum, 'Where is Grandpa Joe?'

Tatum's face lit up as though she had just had a brilliant idea as she repeated the question out loud, "Where is Grandpa Joe?"

I explained to her that Grandpa Joe was in the shop working on a project. I described what he was doing that night.

With another lull in the conversation, Brittany once again, leaned over and whispered a prompt to Tatum.

'How's your knee grandma?' Tatum's face lit up and looked delighted to have another great question to ask.

Tatum repeated the question, "How is your knee grandma?"

I told her it was getting better every day and that I was doing exercises. I flexed my knee a few times for her to see that I was almost as good as new!

If I'm puttering in the kitchen and visiting at the same time, Brittany will say "Whatcha cooking grandma?" And I give a full description of what is happening in my kitchen. Sometimes it spawns a question from Tatum and we become involved in an easy flow. That's what we want ... that nice easy flow back and forth.

Conversation confidence is a tool ... and Brittany is teaching her children something that they will use for the rest of her life ... it goes WAY beyond what a computer screen can teach her. Conversation can be used face to face ... screen to screen ... over the phone.

It can be taken to preschool and middle school;

She can take conversation skills to high school and then college;
she can use it with family and friends;
and she can use it wisely as she tests for her doctorate and then ...
she can take it with her to the company boardroom ... no one will know as they look at the bright confident woman, that she gained her poise from a mom, teaching her how to have a conversation.

All that ... from talking on Facetime with Grandma ...

So, call grandma!

Just One More Thing

It inhabited the musty basement of 1217 Fillmore Street long before I ever met it! The old, dilapidated table and chairs were left for dead in the dark dingy cellar.

One of THOSE things that gets left behind for the next person to haul to the dump. The problem was, I had no truck to haul it to the dump or it would have been gone in a heartbeat.

The caning in the chairbacks were all ripped out and the veneer tabletop was peeling back and was rippling in layers as it collected cobwebs and sheets of dust in the unused basement. I would look at it occasionally and shake my head. I wished I knew somebody who could just haul it to the dump for me.

As new owners, and a newly married couple, Mike and I moved in with all the dreams and hopes of filling this house. The only time I went in the basement was to do laundry. Years went by and the table and chairs accumulated more spider webs and dust and seemed to disappear from my view.

Then one year, I looked at it again.

I questioned and wondered what it would look like in black … I mean really it might not be too bad with a black high gloss sheen … the old table had an old fashioned solid style to it … but what would I do with the warping table top? And the torn and ripped caning in the chairs? Was it crazy to even think about making this old table usable again?

I moved the dump-destined set upstairs … not even believing that I was thinking about using it. At first, I used a tablecloth to hide the veneer and made soft fabric gold velour slip covers to hide the broken chair backs and it looked okay – almost good enough.

One year I decided to **do just one more thing**. Recover the seats, using some new black vinyl and a staple gun. It was simple and easy to do. It was a small thing.

The next summer I decided **to do just one more thing.** Painting the tabletop high glass black. It didn't look too bad but the warping looked awful. So, day after day …. every day at daycare naptime … for months and months … as soon as my daycare children went down for a nap, I quickly brushed a layer of water-based polyurethane on the tabletop. It dried fast, it was summer, and the windows were open so it didn't smell at all … and no one even noticed that the polyurethane was filling in the warps, as the tabletop smoothed out. All summer long, layer after layer, and the warping disappeared.

Another year I decided **to do just one more thing**. I asked an upholsterer to replace the broken woven caning in the chair backs. He said, "I can do it for you, but it's easy! I'll get the supplies for you, and I'll tell you exactly how to do it" ... and he did ... and I did! I was astonished at how easy it was and gratifying at the same time. The webbed caning sheets had to be softened in water and then molded into the chairback frame with a binder strip. My friend was right, it was easy, even for a beginner.

When the caning dried, I painted those chair backs a high gloss white, creating a stunning contrast inside the frame of the high gloss black.

Almost without noticing the entire table set had been refurbished – almost like it was new again and the table became the centerpiece of our home.

I painted the built-in dining room hutch a high gloss black to match the table with high gloss white handles. My new desk was painted outside in the summer in high glass black with white handles ... to match the table & chairs ... and all of it became a comfortable invitation to sit down and stay a while. The ruined and broken-down table and chairs was now the center of my daycare and our home. My very first grandchild Brady used to eat and play table toys with daycare children during his early years.

The old dirty basement was remodeled and turned into a family/play room. The laundry room was updated, and we added a half bath. We had grown and upgraded the house and ourselves along the way … none of it was the same and neither were we. The table and chairs stood proudly in the center, entertaining every person who came to the door. Almost everyone new in the house commented on the stunning table and chairs.

As for the table; it got to be new twice! The first time was its creation when it was originally built and then again decades later when it was found and rediscovered in the dust and the cobwebs of the basement. It was brought back to life by doing just **one more thing**.

I have to admit, for a long time I just wanted somebody to haul it away. Sometimes it's just easier to give up … taking the lazy way out and not thinking about the long range consequences. I'm proud of myself that I could see the potential one step at a time.

Sometimes it's the same with people – making ourself better just by doing one more thing … because you don't realize that you can be new again … and somebody else might just give up on you. The table got a second wind, a time of renewal … and I realized that sometimes the biggest difference in the world … is when someone else sees something in **you** … that even YOU couldn't see at the time.

I couldn't see the whole picture of that table and chair set … but I COULD see the next step – and I try to remember that every day. All I can do today … is … **just one more thing**.

Tate's Hearing

April 14, 2017

For months Joe has been telling me that Tate couldn't hear. I didn't think it could be that bad. But today I opened the garage door and saw Tate, our Shepard husky, sleeping soundly at the head of my garage on a large piece of carpeting. I smiled to myself.

Then I realized that the noise of the garage door had not awoken him. I cautiously pulled my car into the garage so as not to startle him. I got out of my vehicle ... shut the door ... and walked around the back of the car.

Finally, Tate looked up and realized that I was there. How could I have NOT noticed his hearing loss?

I found my mind going back in time when Tate found a beaver under the front deck. He held it tight in his jaw and he knew that he couldn't drop it ... he was in a predicament. If he dropped it, the beaver was going to rip him to shreds. Tate's grip on the animal was nothing short of miraculous –how did he know to grab the beaver right behind the head on the back of the neck? It completely disabled the beaver. Yet at the same time Tate was in bondage too ... he had to keep the beaver in his jaws, or the beaver was going to strike out.

There was only one remedy – Joe knew it ... so did Tate ... the two had to cooperate and work together.

Joe grabbed a shovel and took aim at the head of the beaver ... the beaver was writhing back and forth in constant movement trying to free itself... I didn't want to look. If the shovel hit the beaver it would kill it – if the shovel hit Tate ... well ... somehow this needed to be resolved. Oh geez! I didn't want to look!

It was over before it even started ... the beaver went limp in Tate's mouth while Joe quietly urged Tate to drop the Beaver. The beaver laid helpless on the cement.

Now today with sadness I realized that, if there was a beaver in the yard, Tate wouldn't even know it was there.

Today, I realized that it is *my* time to protect *him*. He's been doing it for me for years without me even thinking about it, without me even noticing. I just have always assumed he is there for my care. When Joe was gone fishing, he would willingly come in the house to sleep near the entrance. Even though he never barked, he always let me know if something or someone was in the yard. Just his sheer size was imposing to someone who had never met him before.

He marked his territory well and it was rare to have any kind of animal wander into our yard.

Tate "the meathead" we called him ... he earned the name; one day when I arrived home from the grocery store with three pork roasts ... I put two in the freezer and was planning one for tomorrow's crock pot meal. When I couldn't find the third one, I assumed I had inadvertently left one at the grocery store - I called to check. The store had not found a pork roast that had been left behind. The next day Joe was cleaning out the kennel and came in with a wrapper from a pork roast. At least Tate had the good manners to look shameful when it was discovered. He was a "meathead" alright!

The day I drove into the garage without Tate hearing me, I should have known that this was no ordinary day. He had chosen this comfortable place to die. Right here with the open air and sunshine flowing all around him and the soft carpet beneath his body. He knew it was time ... Joe and I just didn't want to admit it.

Tate had trusted his instincts as he cared for our property. He loved his life taking care of the woodchucks, rabbits, and even beavers. Now his instincts were telling him it was time to go ... I should have known that it was not cute — not cute at all. We were about to say goodbye to the best country friend Joe ... and I ... and this property had ever known.

He taught us way more than we taught him ... even about dying.

He taught us as he willingly moved on to the next part of his journey ... without struggle ... taking with him ... our unending love ...

The Knife

Saturday June 2017

When Grandpa Ed Weber left the Earth, his prized fish fillet knife was returned to the original giver of the gift, his son Michael. For decades it had been sharpened and used.

In 2017 Michael put it back in circulation, like a coin that just needs to be in use in order to feel needed. The fish cleaning knife along with the love of eating and catching fish was passed down into the hands of the youngest grandson Tom now, on Wall Lake in Minnesota.

The knife itself carries the memories of the Weber's who came before. Maybe it carries the love of fishing and wide open lake space, and the fragrance of fresh evening fishing ... and maybe it carries with it the love of knives. It couldn't possibly be that the love of knives gets passed down from one generation to another ...or could it?

It couldn't possibly be a Weber Thing ... or could it?

****

We all knew that Rob Weber had a **lot** of knives but when we heard him say, "This is my 'going out' knife", we knew he had taken it to a whole new level ... a special tool for specific excursions. Like when other people have beach shoes and work shoes and dress shoes . Instead of shoes, for Rob, it was a knife for each occasion ... a pocket knife, utility knife, survival knife, fillet knife and of course a tactical knife (whatever that means) .

Robbie loves good quality, beautiful knives. He spends time diligently hunting for a knife for each family member, when they reach an age of responsibility. Each one of us who have been gifted a knife now affectionately call them our 'going out' knives, that he has chosen for us.

****

It was Robbie's birthday coming up and I sat with Cameron, Tatum and Taylor alone on the floor asking, "What should we get for Uncle Robbie for his birthday?" I really didn't expect any great answers from these three little people but Cameron (5) very thoughtfully said, " Maybe we could get him a new knife?"

Wow, I didn't know what to say to that! Rob is a connoisseur of knives! For us to buy a new knife for him would be unthinkable in my mind. HOW would you choose a knife for an expert? So I told Cameron, "We can get him a new knife but it has to be JUST THE RIGHT KNIFE ... and that might take a while to find. So, for now, what *else* could we get for Robs' birthday?"

The little grands and I discussed and then decided on many small items that might be of interest to Uncle Robbie. Things like peanut butter pretzels and a new flashlight for playing in the dark, both of which Robbie just might share with his favorite little people.

When Robbie's August birthday arrived, Robbie showed his deep appreciation for the small gifts we had given to him ... it was fun and fine ... but somehow Cameron's suggestion of the knife was still floating around somewhere in my mind.

Months later while traveling in Colorado I saw personalized pocketknives with LOTS of blades and hidden tools that fold in and out – all of it looking so neatly packaged in one handy dandy tool. I just knew it was the right one. The sides of the knife were polished wood, and it had ROB personalized on it. This was exactly what I had been looking for. Something a bit unique and perfect to fill the suggestion that Cameron had come up with on his own.

Now that I had the knife, I was looking for the opportunity to have Cameron give Robbie the gift.

It was 'closing' 'end-of-the-summer' day at the cabin. A play/work day, to button up the cabin and put away lake toys for the summer. When it was time for lunch, I took little Cameron into the back bedroom & reminded him of our discussion several months earlier. I brought out the knife with Rob's name on it, along with tissue paper and tape, giving him the supplies to wrap it himself.

Cam had just recently started preschool and was learning to spell his name with ALL of its letters. CAMERON. A name with Seven letters!

Looking at Rob's name on the knife he said "He only has three? Only three letters in his name?". It was an important piece of information, as he processed how lucky Rob was – I did not tell him that Rob is Robert ... it wouldn't have mattered because it still was not as many letters as Cameron.

He took the tissue wrapping paper and laid the knife in the paper, smoothing it out nice and flat... then he took tape – four long strips of 3M tape – one at a time, making sure the paper was smooth and flat. I was impressed with how precise he was. Cam and I were about to go back to the kitchen with the gift that was wrapped perfectly ... then Cameron CRUSHED all the carefully smoothed gift wrap into his hand and carried it to the kitchen ... I nearly laughed out loud as in a 'hurry-scurry-lunch-is-ready-sort-of-way' he gave Uncle Robbie his real birthday present.

Robbie looked stunned as Cam dropped the package in his hand and went to eat. As Rob opened the package I explained that Cameron really had wanted to get a new knife for him back in August ... and now it was here. Robbie glanced away as his eyes started to fill with tears ... mine did too ... we both thought it was pretty special that Cam had thought of it by himself.

Even though the gift was late, THIS is what Cameron Weber wanted to get for his uncle Robbie Weber for his birthday. I've known Robbie his entire life, and he has been fascinated with knives as long as I can remember. Maybe it's a Weber Thing ... I don't know ... but I do know ... Cameron Weber wanted to give Robbie Weber a knife for his birthday ... and both of the knives ... the old heirloom fish fillet knife and the new engraved 'Rob' pocket knife will stay exactly where they are ... as the years and the decades go by.

And then later ... a very long time from now ... there will be a day, when the fish fillet knife will once again be passed down ... and the new "Rob going out" knife will be gifted to someone else for the very first time.

And maybe the givers of the knifes will have the same twinkle in their eye as Tom's dad, Mike Weber had the day he passed it to Tom ... because maybe ... just maybe ... the knife and the twinkle ... really are ... a Weber Thing.

Take Your Shoes Off

"Take your shoes off." Little Cameron said to me as I stepped into my grandson's home.

"Take your shoes off!" He kept prodding and looking at my feet as if it was urgent that I take them off. They weren't dirty and yet he repeated excitedly several more times; "Take your shoes off! Take your shoes off!"

I looked at his mom for an explanation and she said, "He wants you to stay ... to him if you leave your shoes on then you are only staying on the rug for a minute and leaving again. If you take your shoes off, it means you're going to stay. He wants you to play."

I smile inside ... oh yes ... I came to play.

His little sister Tatum is wearing my bedroom slippers; the ones I keep in the guest bedroom. Later when I was wearing my own slippers Tatum saw the slippers on my feet and she too says to me, "Take your shoes off". If I sneak my feet back into the warm fuzzy slippers when she's not looking, invariably she turns around and says, "Take your shoes off."

This tiny little comment warms my heart as we sit on the floor playing with the teapot that makes a pouring gurgling noise; the toy coffee maker brews a cup and we drink tea and coffee together on the floor. Time is spacious ….

Later when it is time for me to leave their house for the quiet drive back to grandma's house, I find myself pondering what I had just learned … I asked the question; what had I been taught growing up? If someone had their shoes on or off only meant to me that their shoes were dirty or clean. I asked; Did an adult ever come to play with me? No, not ever. I never had an indication that any adult ever **wanted** to play, with me. Maybe more importantly, the adults from my childhood didn't know HOW to play. That was something reserved just for kids.

I used to think, it was kind to just tell a visitor to leave their shoes on in our home**; but** I learned a lesson from my grandchildren.

They are right - without shoes you can sit on the floor and play "tea party" much more effectively. You can sit cross legged and crawl around to find a toy pizza cutter and serve plastic cupcakes on the tray with tea and coffee.

Now when friends or family come to visit, I say, "Take your shoes off" – you are welcome to stay and play 'adult tea party' as long as you like. And I mean it!

Take your shoes off ... sink into my home ... let's sit on the couch or sprawl our legs across an easy chair ... let me bring you a blanket ... and what style slippers would you like me to bring to keep your toes warm? Sit on the floor if you like and let's hoot with laughter! And now tell me how you've changed – and tell me what life has taught you. And I will tell you what I have learned from my grandchildren ... "Take your shoes off!" ... is an invitation to stay ... an invitation to play ... a time to talk while you are saying nothing ... being together with the toys on the floor ... you sitting next to me and me sitting next to you ... and it is a profound compliment ... to be asked to take your shoes off...

Laura My Bunny Lady

8 13 2022

It felt larger than life stepping onto a stage in a place with a legacy like this one. I had no idea I would ever be on a stage in the birthplace of the girl who made the Wizard of Oz famous! Wow! Grand Rapids, MN; the birthplace of Judy Garland.

My first book of stories Travels on The Yellow Brick Road – Lessons Learned on the Path to Oz, was named because of this magical life path ... and the museum in Grand Rapids asked to sell my book. It was 2004 and I was living my dream; doing a motivational keynote called Never Let a Good Thing Go Unsaid.

Speaking was a side interest of mine – not the way I made my livelihood – but this was the way I fulfilled something deep inside of me that had been incubating for a long time. The fear of public speaking is most people's biggest horror, even more prevalent than the fear of death, and here I am, by choice, stepping into the lion's den of fear. That' right! This is my arena! I've got something to prove, and it doesn't involve anybody but me.

It was here that I met Laura for the first time.

Laura?

Who is Laura, you might ask?

At the time I first met her I didn't know that Laura was one of the munchkins from OZ. One of the little people that floats through life looking for all the good things she can find. She listened to my live presentation that day and then Laura bought the CD recording of the same presentation. She wanted to hear the stories again and a CD would let her hear them once more.

She also wanted to know if she could send me some of her writing for me to read and critique – as if she thought I was a writer! Really? I don't consider myself a writer – I am much more a FEELER – attempting to capture a snapshot of the moments that FEEL powerful.

Laura uses dates and events to organize the details that are important to her ... she rattle off dates and times like an electronic calendar on a smart phone for events all along life's path ... I use feelings to sort people and events ... Laura uses dates and times.

Her writing about a bunny arrived in my mailbox. Yes, you read that correctly, she was writing about a bunny. I read the tales and later she and I talked on the phone about the content and the writing quality.

I knew very little about Laura except that she was on a 'Recovery Journey' of some kind and the tales she was writing had parallels to some of her childhood experiences. She was exploring herself on the inside.

Long periods of time went by - years actually – without talking to or hearing from her. I had no idea where her life was taking her, and honestly, I had no idea where my life was taking me either.

The yellow brick road meandered its way through a Great Recession, while I floundered for a while as companies rarely hired motivational speakers. I sort of drifted along like the scarecrow with Dorothy just going along because there wasn't anything better to do.

I had spent decades studying positive mental attitude in order to create keynote material, so now, in my spare time I was reading textbooks about hypnosis and the deeper power of the mind, pondering what direction my life would take.

The magic of hypnosis was intriguing! But hypnosis just seemed so far outside the 'normal' box as a profession! NOBODY is a hypnotherapist ... just the sound of it made me cringe and I wanted to hide. And yet in 2013 my Yellow Brick Road led to the airport boarding a plane for Arizona to go to school and get certified.

I opened an office.

More years went by ... it never crossed my mind to even wonder where Laura was.

At some point I discovered The Women and Spirituality Conference and made my first trip to attend Alone By Myself. (See the story by that name) As the years went by it became an annual thing for a group of girlfriends to spend a weekend traveling and playing together, while attending the conference.

One year I had been thinking about submitting a class proposal for the convention but was too late for the deadline. With my love of public speaking, it was pretty easy to put a last minute class proposal together. I knew there was always a list of last minute additions and deletions each year. So I created a last minute class proposal called, "The Spiritual Side of Hypnosis". I was pretty sure the conference would need a last minute replacement and they did.

At the very same time Laura was standing on the same Yellow Brick Road looking at the last-minute class changes. She saw my name on the page ... she thought there can't possibly be two people with this hyphenated name. She had no expectation that I would recognize her, but the wheels were turning in her head. She had gotten a Ty Beanie Babies Bunny and it was her one creative chance to see if I would be able to put the pieces together and figure out who she was.

She came early to the classroom when I was the only one there before my presentation began. I saw a rather munchkin-like woman with an impish smile approaching.

She looked familiar but I couldn't tell you why. She handed over to me a Beanie Bunny as a memento of our past friendship. She waited and watched while the bunny worked its magic on me. She was watching the wheels in my mind turning, in an effort to put the pieces together.

Laura! How could this be? All these many years had passed ... I hugged her hard. This was too crazy!

In just a few moments my class was starting. I had no time to digest the interaction. Laura sat in the class with rapt attention as I explained to the group the connection between the subconscious mind and spirituality ... that state of mind that is between asleep and awake ... the place we call prayer or meditation ... that active deeper part of the mind that is searching and sending out signals for what we call the Law of Attraction ... attracting situations and circumstances into our lives.

She sat amid the large circle of class attendees. How could this happen? Exactly what I was explaining to the group was happening in real time. Laura and I met in one part of the state at an event and now in a completely different part of the state at an entirely unrelated conference. And why? So many years had gone by, it was almost as if we were meeting in a new lifetime.

Before the class started, I tucked the interaction away in my mind and I would bring it out to mull it over, perhaps on the drive home.

I had no idea why Laura was back in my life, but I soon realized it was her recovery healing journey that brought her and I together in my office in the next few years. The angels themselves directed her healing. What was she recovering from, you might ask?

"LIFE" I would say:

The traumas that stop us in our tracks. -- The times of aloneness in the dark. -- When the depth of our soul feels abandoned. -- Those years of tragedy and not knowing.

And then ...

She began to feel her strength. -- And she began to feel some power, perhaps for the first time. -- And the feeling of caring and love was introduced like a foreign language. -- And she began to ask 'how to feel love' -- How to welcome love.

Giving love to others is second nature to me ... it flows through me like a waterfall ... I couldn't stop it if I wanted to. How could one live any other way?

Unknowingly and innocently, I handed Laura copies of my first and second book. I had no expectations of a response from the books.

The next day this email arrived.

Hi Cathy

Too much in my heart for one email, but here is a start. I have just spent the last 90 minutes sitting in my car in the parking lot where I live. I could not stop reading until I got to page 110. Then I knew I would send this email. In the spirit of : Never Let a Good Thing Go Unsaid," this comes your way.

I sit here in the community room where I have access to one of the two computers for residents to use. With face buried in my hands I remember to breathe before sharing this. Monday after I left your office, I went to the parking lot outside of the Jo Ann Fabrics store there in Alexandria. Sitting alone in my car, I selected at random three entries to read from your second book. My heart was so overwhelmed by those nuggets of memorable moments, that without sensor, I spoke these words: "I love you, Cathy." Those words came from my spirit to yours. Because we had talked, I felt safe in allowing myself to not only experience the emotion that welled up, but to give words that labeled what I felt OUT LOUD! It was about how I felt being given the gift of those moments that you had put to paper. To experience a part of your heart put in print for others to see. I am so blessed by the gift that the Universe gave to me by bringing us together at this point in time.

Page 76 also resonates with me. I live at Wellstone Commons here in Northfield, where Mr. Wellstone taught at Carlton College. This affordable public senior housing was named after him. Of the five different public housing locations I have lived since June 2002, this one is the nicest and the newest. I live on the main floor in the Northwest corner, so I have windows on two walls in the living room and nine-foot ceilings. The frosting on the cake is a fixed window over the kitchen sink and a 30" electric stove. (In Ely my first stove was 20', so the pots touched each other. I had an opportunity to get a 24" stove later when I moved from 2nd floor to the 1st floor. Much better, but my roaster pan for the Thanksgiving turkey wouldn't fit in the oven.) No problem here loving my 30" stove.

Best close now. Blessings & Hugs

****

I don't know how many years ago it was when I received this email ... Laura would know. Now I read this message and see WAY more than I saw at the time.

When I met Laura, I had no idea that she was starving.

That may sound like a strong statement, but she was starving.

She and I worked together in the office doing healing work and she did her own personal healing work in between trips to Alexandria ... lots of work – mountains of work - with forgiveness. She did the hard inner work ... step by step ... and as she trudged through the muck and the mire ... when it would get really deep, she would come to me ... and my love and the angels' love would pull her out of the quicksand that was threatening to pull her down.

All I did was keep on loving her, without thinking ... and unbidden ... an automatic replenishing supply. Laura was going from feeling alone to feeling loved. It did not shock or surprise me on the day Laura responded to my love statement ... the day she said she loved me too. Why would I be surprised by love?

And then the tipping point came. Remember in the Wizard of OZ movie when everything turns from BLACK & WHITE to full vibrant COLOR?

That's what happened to Laura ... reading in the parking lot that day. The day that love became so strong, it outweighed all of the PAST. The day the angels gave her the stories she needed to read ... first in the Alexandria parking lot and then later in the parking lot at her home.

The FEELING of LOVE in the stories is when it all came tumbling down. You see, Laura **wasn't starving for MY love** ... Laura was starving to **love herself**.

As she sat in the car saying "Cathy, I love you" she wasn't opening up to me – I had always been open to her ... she was opening up to herself ... **Laura was FEELING along with my stories** ... MY stories of love opened Laura up to **her own stories** of love. Those tiny keepsake moments that we sometimes overlook, not realizing that minute by minute - even second by second , there is love in our lives.

Her world turned from Black & White to Technicolor; it was almost imperceptible and monumental at the same time.

NOW she could FEEL HER OWN stories. She could FEEL her own love.

Nothing had changed ... and yet her entire life shifted inside herself ... it took years ... and yet it happened in a moment. Going from Black & White to Technicolor made all the difference in the world ... Laura had learned to love herself.

"Yes Dorothy, you've always been able to go home, you just had to learn it for yourself."

Surprise Surprise Surprise!

Phoenix, Arizona

"I'm sorry mom but I can't go. I just can't make it fit, I have to be in the Twin Cities for work that weekend." That's what he had said to me. It was such a complete and concise response, that looking back, I should have been suspicious.

All I wanted was to have my three sons together. We were all going to be at John's house in AZ and if Tom could fly out as well, we could all be together for the weekend.

I had no indication that there was a surprise in store for me – none.

The desert of Arizona was spewing out heat just as fast as the grill that was heating outside on the patio. After getting off the plane and being welcomed by family I was urged to step outside onto the patio. And a second time, I was even encouraged to go outside. Finally, I stepped outside ... surprise! Surprise! surprise!!!

Tom stepped out of the shadows on the dark patio, the surprise was totally a gift to me! This mom had all three of her babies together!

****

The musical group had come all the way from Japan. The recent earthquake tsunami disaster their entire nation faced was the first question we had at the reception in their honor. Were their families safe? They have been deeply touched by the inquiries as they toured the United States. Even the young students they had entertained at our local elementary schools asked about their loved ones back home.

The entire group went to the winery for socializing following the initial greeting reception. Joe and I chatted with local acquaintances, and I asked Joe if he wanted to sit at a table where two people had a table for four.

"Yes, let's sit with them." he said, "She works at the county, I know her."

I sat and introduced myself to the quiet woman on my left. We searched for commonalities and found few. She knew that I had done daycare for years and that I was licensed through the county. We listened intently to one song and then returned to our conversation. This quiet woman, near stranger, turned to me and said,

"I met your son."

"Really?" I said. I was surprised.

"Yes" she said, "at a conference in the Twin Cities." She continued, "I was walking among the vendors when a young man saw my name tag from Douglas county!"

"Douglas county!" he said, "I grew up in Douglas County! And I'm flying to Arizona tomorrow to surprise my mom!". Tom told her the whole story. She knew that I had asked him to come to Arizona to make our family complete at John and Shannon's in Arizona ... his two brothers would be there, and it would be so nice if he could come and spend the weekend. He told her the part about his excuse of needing to be at the conference and his upcoming surprise for me ...

Before she left his vendor booth Tom said teasingly, "Now don't you tell my mom!" What a cute thing for him to say to a complete stranger!

I listened to the almost stranger ... at this small town event ... telling me a story about meeting my son ...

In a moment we were no longer strangers ...she was no longer quiet and shy ... from one mother to another ... we sat close to each other – letting the background noise fade away, as we talked about our children.

I knew she had been putting herself in my place when Tom told her about the weekend. She was feeling what it was going to be like – when he stepped out of the shadows on the patio ... when one mom got the gift of having all of her sons in one place ... at one time ... once again.

... THAT is why she remembered my son – she knew how it would feel for me ... she kept it and saved it in her memory ... put it in a safety deposit box for 15 months ... dusted it off and brought it out ... over a glass of wine ... two strangers savoring the delightful flavor of motherhood.

Lemonade Stand

"I will guard it with my life " I heard the woman say.

When I went to pay for my item at the garage sale, I asked the woman, "What are you going to guard with your life?"

She smiled and said "Oh, my daughter's lemonade stand."

I smiled. There are a lot of lemonade stands this time of year.

I said to the woman "I saw a beautiful thing yesterday". She looked at me as though she was urging me to go on. And so, I did.

I told her, "I was about a block away from the library when I saw a little girl with a lemonade stand. A police car pulled up across the street and parked."

" You could see that the little girl at the lemonade stand was looking a little bit nervous. The police officer got out of his car, and was crossing the street toward her. The uniform seemed to make her a little bit uneasy. Heading toward her, he intentionally reached his hand into his pocket to pull out some money. You could visibly see the little girl's body relax." I said to the woman, "Then another police car pulled up and parked behind the first car and both of them came to buy lemonade."

She looked at me and said exactly what I was thinking. "Why would anyone want to live anywhere else besides here? We have such wonderful people! People who are always willing to help others! " Her face beamed!

I nodded my head in agreement.

She told me that she was riding bicycle with her daughters a few weeks ago and a police officer pulled over near them. He put the window down and congratulated the young girls on wearing their helmets while they were riding their bikes. And then he gave them each a sticker. Her face was filled with such warmth and appreciation for what we have.

I don't know how much money the little girl by the library made that day, but I know her Return-On-Investment was way above average for a one-day business venture.

The police officer knows that it begins with them ... just like any other relationship ... begins with just one ... one person doing the right thing, in the right way, at the right time. I wonder if those officers really like lemonade, or if they are like me, having no intention of drinking the beverage ... lemon might not be their flavor of choice.

Could it be while buying lemonade they are, at the same time, distributing their own flavor of a thirst quencher we don't even realize we need? ... to quench our thirst for safety? As if to say, "Yes, my job involves some bad things, like you see on TV, but that's the smallest part of my job." And maybe the BIGGEST part of my job ... is supporting and encouraging good kids and good people ... so we are focusing on – what we want to keep growing.

The police officer is most likely a daddy too ... wanting only for us ... exactly what he wants for his own children ... to have a lemonade stand on the street ... and a feeling of comfort and safety ... and a small town feeling of peace ...

Super Hero

9 15 2022

It was just a moment ...nothing spectacular ... just a moment I captured. The car battery was dead.

It doesn't matter how the battery got dead, I just know I was not the cause of it – thank God!

The hood was up, and I was in the front passenger seat checking my phone messages while Joe was attending to the issue at hand. There was nothing else for me to do.

Joe had sent for help from an unlikely guy – my ex-husband. Yes, you read that right. Mike is not a repair kind of person, and he will tell you that. Mike willingly takes a back seat on any kind of repair project, and lets someone else be in charge. He gives others a wide berth, letting them know this is not his area of expertise.

But today, as we are stranded in the lower Cedar Building parking lot, Mike is the person Joe called for assistance. Mike has a gadget – one of those things everybody should have – an instant jump start! Not only did he HAVE the gadget ... but he would be here in THREE

MINUTES!!!! Mike is more than happy to bring his toy to the sandbox and play.

I gave him a welcoming hug as he arrived, and then left the two of them to figure this out. I knew for sure; I had nothing to add.

Casually, I sat in my car ... while the hood was up. I could see only about five inches between the raised hood and the base of the car...just enough to see two bodies standing in front of my car working together... I see them through the windshield. I have no concern ... I know they will resolve this without me.

With Mike's new gadget, the car starts instantly.

Joe is usually the fix-it hero ... the one that gets called to put on the Superhero cape in a time of need. Today Mike was the hero. But neither one of them cares who wears the cape ... they can switch it up ... in that comfortable relaxed moment, I wished for others to experience what I have ... my husband and my ex-husband working together ... side by side ... chatting and joking ... enjoying the moment ... and most of all ... enjoying each other.

Like a Good Neighbor

7 21 2015

I sat up straight in my office chair as I read the email – my chest was swelling with pride … I could feel my heart pounding as I read it. What my youngest son wrote took my breath away. Tom lives in Fargo ND and is a State Farm agent.

This is what he said.

Subject Line: Joe Formusa

I have to share a story with you. When I was in training (to become a State Farm Agent) one week in the Twin Cities, probably February of 2014, our Area Vice President- Joe Formusa spoke to our class. He would be Dick's boss's boss. He oversees 80 Sales Leaders and 2,500 Agents across 13 states. He talked about his role with the company and then at the end he said what he enjoys most is going around with Sales Leaders and visiting new agents. And he said he doesn't just visit any agencies; he only goes to the **best of the best**. He said if you ever see me in your office, you should consider it a compliment. Fast forward to today, July 21st 2015 ... Three men in suits just left my office ... one of which was Joe Formusa, who flew to Fargo because he wanted to meet me and Ryan Kill. I'm humbled and honored that he came, so of course I had to share it with my mom 😊 Love you tons.

Tom Weber, Agent

I sat at my computer taking in the magnitude of what I had just read. I could only imagine what that must have felt like for him, knowing that these three men in suits flew in to Fargo ND to tell my son he is one of the **best of the best** that State Farm has. To take the time and energy to personally step into the office was monumental.

In a time when , Zoom is so much easier ... and THAT is the whole point! Zoom is easy. It's like sending a quick insignificant text message when a handwritten card arriving in the mail has a permanent effect. You know what I mean! When something physical comes in the mail; it's tangible – you can touch it – you can look at it again and again – it lays on the desk or the table and every time you look at it, it feels better and better. THAT is what happened to my son that day ... something tangible.

I'm a mom watching from the sidelines, and I wanted Joe Formusa to know, that I appreciated this monumental moment ... I wanted him to know that I ... yes, me his mother ... knew that he had gone above and beyond to help my son be successful ... gone above and beyond to help Sate Farm be the icon it has become.

So, I decided to try to find Joe Formusa. I checked social media with no success. After looking around the web, I finally got in touch with a STATE FARM person who KNEW Joe, so I figured 'what do I have to lose?' I sent a simple note that said; I would like get ahold of this gentlemen. I didn't' say WHY I wanted to get in contact with him ... no details whatsoever.

I was shocked to receive a friendly and yet cordial response within a few hours saying that they would forward my message to Joe! Wow! That was impressive!

Then in less than 24 hours I received an email directly from Joe himself!

I told Joe: "I am a mother who is in the process of writing my third book of stories. Those small, monumental moments that can be life-changing, defining moments. I told him that I take notes of these day-to-day small events in my computer when they happen; and these precious moment files accumulate as the years go by, without me even noticing. Then, just when I think I should delete the whole bunch –saying to myself that ' I'm never going to have time to write stories again' ... I sit down and read the files and weep at the beauty in my life.

Well, yesterday I opened a file from 2015 from my son in Fargo ND. I wanted to share it with you; **because YOU are the very person that created this monumental**

moment for my son. And I am EVER grateful. I forwarded the email above to Joe.

This was the response that came back from Joe Formusa
Thank you for this, Cathy! You made my day- week- year!
Tom accurately remembers what I said, and you have described how I was trying to motivate the team. I have been retired as a senior executive for almost seven years and those days I spent visiting agents like Tom are my favorite memories and still make me smile. I appreciate you for reaching out and giving me the best gift ever.
Happy Writing!
Joe

I sighed as I read his message to me. It's a two-way street. Joe gave confidence and encouragement to my son when he needed it most ... every person that has helped my sons along the way is on my list to say THANK YOU.

I call Joe a multiplier. Joe knows that he didn't make it to his level of success by himself; there were people that helped him like he had helped my son; and now it's payback time! Like a good neighbor he is helping every single person that he can! I'm betting he is one of those people that spends his life boosting the self-esteem of others ... encouraging and motivating hundreds, maybe even thousands of agents, and in turn, they multiply and pass that really good feeling on to others.

Joe gets it; there is nothing more impactful than being there in person ... yup you can get on a Zoom call ... but when three men in suits physically arrive in your office, after getting off an airplane ... in a small regional airport

... for one purpose ... to meet you ... THAT makes an impression. THAT makes you work harder. THAT makes you determined to prove that you are WORTH IT! To prove that you are every bit, the person Joe Formusa came to see that day.

You know that these three men ... shoulder to shoulder ... were a powerhouse stepping off that plane. I can't even imagine the energy in the room as the office door swung open on the unsuspecting staff as well as my son that day. What does it feel like to look up ... know that these three have come to meet you personally ... on your turf ... in your office. There can be nothing better than physically hearing the words echoing right there in your office ... the sound Joe Formusa's voice ringing off the walls ... seeing the facial expressions as the three men in suits meet your staff ... and to feel a real handshake ... feeling the support and camaraderie ... it's way more than a screenshot ... it's way more than electronics can provide ... it's a memory of a lifetime ... an experience; a face to face message that says loud and clear ...
you matter ...
you are here for **us** ...
we are here for **you** ...
like a good neighbor ...   State Farm is there.

Substitutions

Last night I stood at my kitchen counter shaping crushed Oreo cookies and cream cheese into perfect little balls. I set them outside to cool in the cold of Minnesota, while the dipping chocolate was melting on the stove. And all the while as I stood at the counter, my iPad was propped up against the backsplash. On the screen was my granddaughter Maggie, across the country in Arizona. She and I were baking together. She was making a recipe of M & M cookies.

I asked her if she had ever just put the whole batch of cookie dough on a cookie sheet and baked them as cookie bars ... she was quiet for a second ... and then I could see the light bulb clicking ON above her head.

She thought that sounded much easier! So she tried spreading the dough on a cookie tray with a spatula and I said, "Look here, at this big spoon - get one of these and use it like this." I motioned to her to use the back of the spoon to spread the thick dough. "Oh" she said, "that works better". We said goodbye as she popped the pan in the oven.

When the bars were nearly done she FaceTimed again and said, "Are these done grandma?"

"Well, let's look" I said. She held her phone in front of the glass oven door. "No, not quite. About another 10 minutes".

Later, when they were cooled, I received a photo by text message of her bars, neatly cut and stacked on a plate, just like a baking website photo.

It is quite a common scene for the two of us to be together like this, me chopping vegetables and she on the other end ... two electronic devices connecting us as we chatter on for minutes and half-hours.

We create secrets during our time together. Things we don't tell other people; and we learn things together too. I have a secret, want to hear it? Will you promise not to tell?

One time on Facetime ... we made substitutions to Maggie's chosen recipe. Yup, just the two of us electronically baking together. A professional baker might cringe at our shenanigans! One of our secrets that night was that we used Orville Redenbacher Popping oil in a triple layer chocolate cake. We were diligently focused and working together and figuring it out when Maggie looked at me and said, exactly what I was thinking, "Grandma, this is *almost* like *being together*". I could feel my eyes starting to get wet ...

We forged on - making changes to the somewhat complicated recipe. Not only did the substitutions work, but Maggie's parents and friends raved about the creation. Maggie's' cake was perfect and no one suspected any replacements.

An electronic connection made all of this possible. It's a substitute for when I can't be there ... it allows me to hang out with Maggie ... face to face ... seeing her expressions ... blowing her a kiss ... waving good bye ... telling her I love her... feeling the closeness ... and sensing the nearness.

I cried a few tears after I closed the cover on the iPad. At first, I thought the tears were sadness. However, I was wrong. They were tears of gratitude. Because every time I hear the iPad ring ... I just want to thank the Steve Jobs' of the world, for the marvelous devices that connect us in a nanosecond. As Maggie's face pops up on the screen, I want to thank someone for letting me be with my granddaughter as she cleans her room.:-) I want to shout with joy that I can check the cookie bars in her oven from 1600 miles away. When I text her during her school day, I know that later I will see her smiling face. And we can do all that ... only because we are living in this time.

Oh of course,
... I'd rather BE with Mags.
    ... I'd rather crawl into bed beside her and wrap my arms around her.
       ... I'd rather kiss her face until she screams for mercy.

But ... either way we are face-to-face.
      ... either way, we feel the nearness.
        ...either way, we are together.

   Wishing you ... togetherness.   Cathy & Joe

***This story is printed with Maggie's permission to share one of our baking secrets.

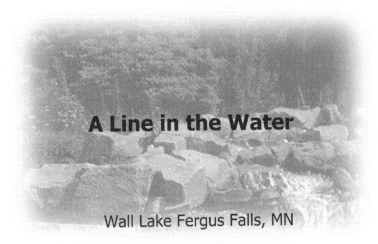

A Line in the Water

Wall Lake Fergus Falls, MN

7 16 2022

It was a floating party to be exact. Rock With the Dock Out!! That's what it is.

This is people-watching at its finest! It's a party going on with people who don't normally smoke begging a cigarette from a total stranger, just because this is a place to let your hair down. It is the magic of a Minnesota July on the sandbar – a small community of boats, pontoons and jet skis gathering on the sandbar; with people that have been friends and neighbors, for a long time ... or a short time ... it doesn't matter.

A band plays floating on a pontoon in the middle of a lake, with a floating bar right next to it. Tailgating on the water ... people grilling food and appetizers ... pans of food being passed around and burgers being offered to others – there is always more than enough to go around. This party was going to continue beyond the setting of the sun.

At about 3:45 our littlest grandbaby Taylor needed a nap. I am the designated napping assistant known as Grandma. I am more than willing to go back to the cabin and sit quietly as she sleeps ... and perhaps ... maybe just maybe ... I might just wrap myself up with a blanket in the chill of the air conditioning to take a little snooze myself. Ah, the loveliness of a nap ... and afterwards she and I can go back and join the party again.

She went to bed willingly and so did I – she in the crib and me on the sofa.

Later, I sat up from my snooze on the sofa, glanced outside and looked across the lake. I've heard of drawing a line in the sand, but what I was watching out the window was a line in the water. This is only the second time I have ever seen this, both times were on Wall Lake.

The rain was pounding its way across the surface of the lake. My eyes were locked on the sight, trying to figure out WHAT I was seeing. The cloud coming across the lake was dropping water so rapidly and in such large quantities on the lake, that it looked like a literal line in the water moving across the surface of the water coming toward the cabin. On one side of the line there was complete calm before the rain came and the other was utter chaos as the buckets of water from the cloud overhead dumped and bounced on the surface of the lake. The line of rain was getting closer to our cabin now and I could only imagine what was happening back at the sandbar with a CLOUDBURST like this.

As I looked across the water, I saw pontoons and boats at full speed heading to their respective homes and cabins, trying to beat the rain! It was easy for me to pick out our family's pontoon heading directly for our cabin. As the pontoon docked, there was a mad dash to get everyone inside the cabin and get out of the storm.

With water dripping and wet clothes & towels, they came inside and all huddled together at the windows watching the wall of water continue across the lake. The sheer power of the raincloud was breathtaking.

"What had happened to the band and to their equipment?" I asked.

They said that when the rain came, there was instantly a hand-to-hand brigade formed. The band's musical equipment, rapidly, one item at a time, was being passed, from one person to another ... getting it first to land ... and then into a vehicle. A construction worker had emptied his tools from his truck and let the tools sit in the rain to get wet, in order to save and transport the musical equipment from the sandbar, up the big hill, past the playground and up to the lodge. In minutes the musical equipment was relocated to the Elks Lodge and set up near the dance floor. Wow!

They were telling me the story as we stood in the cabin listening intently to the sound of Mother Nature. When the downpour turned to a gentle regular rain, Little Miss Taylor woke up from her nap. Everyone else was toweled off and redressed in dry clothes. We continued the summer day, in a different location as we joined the party at the lodge.

The organizer of the event said it was a thing of beauty, watching all that equipment being handed from one person to another and all of it in smooth cooperation ... everyone walked away soaked and happy as if nothing out of the ordinary had happened.

And everyone would be right.

We play together and if it rains, we work together ... and then we play some more.

It really **wasn't** anything out of the ordinary. It happens all the time in a million different ways. People working together ... that feeling of oneness that is just a part of all of us ... there's a plant sale going on in my office building for Elder Network ... same thing - yesterday as if by magic, boxes of plants were being dropped off ... it happens so often and so frequently ... that it goes without notice.

The party on the water began with playing in the sun and changed when the rain came ... everyone helped get out of the rain ... down to the lodge with the band set up once again ... now the music was floating out the windows ... telling the rain to continue at its own pace ... we were sharing connection and food and good music and some cocktails ... once again ... adults and children once again ... just a different location.

No one gets mad at the line in the water ... the rain on one side and the sun on the other ... the rain and the sun are both welcome ... the adults and the children are both welcome ... we are just here to play together and work together ... nothing more ... everybody helping everybody ... it's a mighty nice feeling ... people and nature ... having a party together.

Spilled Soup

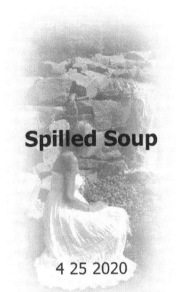

4 25 2020

The potato soup was warming on the stove. I made it yesterday and brought it along to Fargo today. Tommy ladled warmed soup into a bowl and handed it to 4-year-old Cameron who was taking it to the dining table.

I watched as he wobbled a bit trying to focus on the soup. It overflowed the edge of the bowl onto the floor. Instantly there were tears and crying. Tommy looked over and said, "We don't cry over spilled soup Buddy". Tommy grabbed a terry towel from the counter as though it were a magician's silk scarf magically floating through the air. Like a performer he simply swabbed up the warm soup into the towel and gracefully lifted it into the sink … and the little boys' tears stopped.

With the bowl of soup now on the table, Cameron took a small stack of crackers and crushed them over the top of the soup. The look of surprise on his dad's face made it obvious he had never seen his son do this. Tommy said, "Well, I guess you've done that before!"

Little Tatum girl said in a singsong tone, "Tommy! Tommy!" ... this little grand girl had heard me calling him Tommy. Watching Tommy making a sandwich for Cam, I said in a meaningful way, "Your kids won the lottery". He smiled. We both knew it was true.

Cameron will remember the gentle daddy voice who said so calmly, "We don't cry over spilled soup Buddy".

The essence of life gets passed down in those tiniest of little particles ... those moments of wiping up the soup and expressing love at the same time ... what will they remember? Will they remember the soup?

No ... but yes. They won't remember the specific bowl of soup. They won't remember the specific time with a fever. They won't remember the specific time they scraped their knee. They won't remember how young and handsome their daddy is right now. They won't remember how sexy and beautiful their mamma is right now.

But they will remember the thousands of love moments. Those particles that add up to a feeling ... a knowing actually ... that ... there are two people who walk the earth ... that love them unconditionally.

Two people who will move mountains to take care of them ... two people who sit each evening with arms wrapped around four little offspring ... saying clearly without words ... you are safe ... you are loved ... and you are never alone.

Little Yellow Dress

It was a delightful little thing that I wasn't sure I would even be able to wear. I found the yellow sundress at a garage sale. I paid $1 for it.

It was strapless with a blousy kind of top and then elastic gathers at the waist. The skirt had two layers of gathered ruffles that bounced with each step. And even though it was quite an appropriate length as it came down just above the knee, it had a sexy flouncy air about it as the skirt swished back and forth.

It was the end of July and my naturally dark skin had turned to a deep golden brown color, like my dad used to have each summer. The yellow dress was a stunning contrast to the dark mocha skin color.

Joe's brother was visiting and joining us for the family reunion on Lake Miltona that was coming up.

I was tempted to wear ordinary typical casual clothes but as I was lying in bed I decided to wear the yellow sundress . Just the thought of it made me FEEL good.

At the reunion the son of our hostess was given the job of taking photos and I noticed for the first half hour, that everywhere I went he was taking my photo. No doubt about it, he was taking my photo ... when you feel just a little bit sexy and you feel just a little bit young, you also feel just a little bit special ... that energy floats out from you and it attracts other people.

Two women in their eighties at the reunion remarked "You look young " ... and I felt young and free as a matter fact.

Maybe I would have felt that beautiful that day anyway, but it changes everything when you take a few minutes to look better. So, I bounced around at that family reunion the entire day feeling a delightful sense of vibrancy.

Later we stopped at the Eagles Club where there was a band playing ... two gentlemen in the crowd smiled at me whenever they were near. One of them looked at me with beautiful twinkles in his eyes, as if they were saying, "Oh yes, you are bright tonight!"

And after we got home Joe's Brother Jim said that two women were coming in from outside the club – most likely having a cigarette outside on the deck; One said to the other "I love that dress she's wearing. "

Just a little thing. Just a dollar. The return on that investment is beyond the high hopes of a Warren Buffett investment. I have no idea what my age was that day and it didn't matter, there are just times when it is YOUR day and YOUR turn to feel REALLY GOOD – on top of the world as a matter of fact.

I almost didn't put the story in this book ... what would my mother say about me talking about myself like this? It might seem shameful in some way.

But I remember a night as a child, when my mother was getting all gussied up to go somewhere. She was putting her bright red lipstick on. I told her "Mommy you're pretty". She smiled down at me and then said the obligatory 'Oh no!' Someone had taught her that you don't accept a compliment ... or you'll get a big head.

I have no idea what my mom's age was that day, and it didn't matter, that was HER day and HER turn to feel REALLY GOOD – on top of the world as a matter of fact. I bet my mom was feeling young and free that night too ... just like my day in the little yellow dress ... I bet my mom knew that feeling ... and I bet she wanted me to feel just as pretty.

The only difference between my mom and I; is that I am printing this story ... telling the world about an extraordinary day in a little yellow dress ... and with each compliment ... I am saying 'Thank you'.

"Slow Slow Slow"
December 13 2014

"Slow" " Slow" "Slow" – I gasped in between each word – as my husband slid my legs across the bed, where my walker waited. Yes, a walker...

I had been trying to remove a cat from a wet slippery floor and ended up with a pelvic fracture, an ambulance, a three-day hospital stay ... a two week stint on drugs that made me realize why addiction happens ... and six weeks of unrequested down time. I wonder who _exactly I will be_ at the other end of this six weeks...

I rarely do anything slowly in my life and now I was forced to be quiet and to heal.

As our son Tommy (Yes I still call him Tommy) embarked on months of training in preparation to open his own insurance agency, Joe and I had told him that weekdays Monday through Friday, we would be taking care of his two Yorkshire terriers, Mason and Murray. Tommy was going to be in a hotel out of town while training and none of us wanted the dogs in a kennel all that time. The very first week of my recovery Tommy insisted that dogs go to a kennel – I was just newly home from the hospital, but of course I had to agree. I was not capable of handling two dogs my first two weeks. Poor babies, I hated the thought.

Finally after two weeks I was beginning to feel human and capable again. It was getting cold outside, and the two dogs came to my house but could not go outside alone.

Mason and Murray were a powerful incentive to get me up and moving and back on my feet. I thought there would be no way I would be able to play with a tennis ball with Mason. Mason was not-stop energy but I couldn't bend over even in a seated position to pick up the ball. But Mason was determined. He brought the ball back to me by jumping up on the couch and dropping it right there on the sofa ! Easy Peasy ... game on! Let's play!

The dogs were so patient. They waited and watched every slow methodical step with the walker. Several weeks into his agency training, Tom asked me why Mason and Murray go around my car twice in the garage before they go out the walk-in door?

 I told him; When they first came, I was using a walker, it took me so long to get down four steps and across the garage, to open the door for them, that they made two laps around my car before I could let them out. They were killing time ... being patient with me ... Tom looked sad when I explained how slow I was with a walker. I didn't want him to feel sorry for me — I wasn't feeling sorry for myself ... I was getting better every day!

The comfort these two little friends brought to me was immeasurable. They slept in the recliner and rested as I read and healed. Murray curled up in a ball next to me and Mason stretched out on the length of my calves when my feet were held up by the recliner. Every afternoon we napped that way.

They gave me a feeling of being needed even as I was almost helpless myself. They brought me immense comfort and unconditional love in my lap. They were patient with everything as I moved with a walker ... getting better and stronger all the time.

Transitioning out of a walker was hard; the walker had become a protection around me. Joe bought me a cane with sunflowers on it and the first time I used it was at a wedding where I had been asked to do the prayer before the meal. I felt more vulnerable than I had ever felt in my entire life. So many people around! I wished I had the walker to keep people back and away from my healing body. The DJ was so kind to notice the cane. Instead of asking me to come to the front to pray — he brought the microphone to me. I was grateful.

This healing time taught me many things ... about compassion for others ... about walking into a room feeling vulnerable ... about being dependent on the kindness of others.

I learned the depth of feeling having an animal ... like having love in my lap ... the rhythm of their breathing as they slept with me ... they urged me to play ball with them ... filled my day with the warmth. What may have seemed like a big commitment, taking care of the dogs, became my saving grace.

When I went back to work, I missed my time during the day with Mason and Murray. They were never mad that I hadn't been home for the morning ... they just rolled with life ... when I arrived home at some point mid-day, the two happy yorkies were ready to go outside. They were curious about the smells from the grocery bags I toted inside.

Eight months I got to have them; I am forever grateful to these two little friends ...they loved my physical therapy exercises on the floor ... they kept me moving tossing balls ... I am not the same person I was before that six-week period of healing ... and I appreciate beyond words that Mason and Murray loved me back to health.

It was never a burden caring for them ... not ever.

I hope they can say the same for me ...

Where Did I Leave My Car?

There used to be times coming out of Wal-Mart, looking at the sea of cars; I had no idea where I left my car. I have seen other people in this lot walking from row to row, sheepishly admitting that they can't find their car.

That all ended for me the day I mentioned it to my son Robbie. He told me that he always parks in the **same** row, the one straight out from the main doors. At the time that he created this habit, he worked a late evening shift and much of his grocery shopping was done around midnight. He took all the guesswork out of it and knew **every time** where to look. So, I adopted that habit, and I've never lost my car since.

One day I was stepping into the warmth of the sun leaving the air conditioning of Walmart behind. I noticed a couple who appeared to be in their early to mid-eighties walking around with a fully loaded shopping cart looking lost. He was pushing the cart, as the two of them were looking worried, confused and a little scared. I was carrying a small bag in each hand.

I stopped in front of them, stretched out my arms a bit and with a reassuring BIG SMILE on my face said, "Let me guess! You can't find your car!"

With a look of worry and concern on their faces, they both said 'yes'.

"It happens to me all the time!!" I said brightly! I was hoping to get a little bit of a smile to help them relax – no deal. I don't know how long they had been in this predicament before I arrived, but they looked exhausted.

To begin the process of elimination I asked them, "Which door did you use to go into the store?"

Well, they thought they had gone in the main food area. We started looking at cars and I asked for details. The car is a burgundy wine color. I looked down one row of parked vehicles and saw five burgundy cars all parked next to each other, different styles and models and asked if any of those were theirs. They said no.

And so, we walked. Now they changed their mind and said they may have gone in the **garden center** doors, so we walked all the way down to the other end of the parking lot looking for burgundy cars. I tried to stay at their slower pace, so that they wouldn't feel alone. We had been walking for 5 to 10 minutes when the woman said to me, "Our license plate starts with 911."

Well, that was a different story! Now I knew it was going to be easy to find the car. I had been trying to walk slowly, to stay with them, but finally I left them behind. We needed to resolve this soon; I needed to find their car, because I could see the escalating concern on their faces.

I took off by myself, walking rapidly across the parking lot quickly scanning for burgundy cars and checking license plates. When she remembered the license plate numbers we had been all the way down by the garden center in row 10. Methodically I kept checking burgundy cars row by row.

Finally, I looked across aisle 4 from a distance ... I thought that I could see 911 on the license plate. And sure enough ... there it was. I raised my hand to the couple and the two of them eventually came up behind me and were delighted to have located their burgundy car with the beginning numbers 911 on the license plate. They looked exhausted and relieved at the same time.

I suggested that maybe from now on they should park right next to a cart corral so that it's 1) easy to find your car; 2) easy to unload groceries and; 3) easy to return the shopping cart right into the cage ... the woman looked at me as though that was a golden idea. The gentleman started unloading their groceries into the trunk.

I don't know who they were ... don't know where they live ... and it didn't matter. They were lost in plain view of a hundred other cars and lots of people they didn't know. They needed a son or daughter to lend a helping hand – and that day it was my pleasure to be a daughter in their time of trouble ... it was big thing to them.

I was about to go to my car when the short, small-framed woman opened her arms and took me in a long slow hug and said, "You are my angel today".

It's not every day, you get to be someone's angel. I had just been promoted from daughter to angel! I like that!

As I walked to my car, I felt like a daughter. That feeling created an ache ... a big ache ... that made me miss my parents. That could have been my mom and dad in that parking lot in their later years. Two perfectly capable people who just got turned around that day ... having an off day and feeling a bit vulnerable ... just needing some help and direction in a massive parking lot.

I waved to them as I walked slowly to my car. I slid onto the seat and there was a yearning in my heart with tears streaming down my face. I sat there ... wishing I could have my mom and dad back for just an afternoon ... just one more time ...

20 minutes earlier I had been helping a couple find their lost car ... I didn't realize their dilemma was an enormous gift to me ...

I had been given the gift of someone needing me and the feeling in my heart right now was golden. I didn't think I was the one that was lost ... and yet as I left the parking lot ... with a glow in my heart ... I felt that I had been found.

Hero Day

I didn't know I was going to be a HERO today. You just never know ahead of time when something monumental is going to happen. Maybe I should buy a Wonder Woman cape to put in my closet!

Brittany said, 'Lets go to the thrift store!' That doesn't sound monumental at all.

Sure ... of course ... four children under the age of five ... 1 mom 1 grandma (me) 2 full size strollers and 2 scooters and 1 baby six weeks old sleeping in my stroller. It will be great exercise for the adults and the baby there was not a peep out of her. She loved the idea of being strolled for blocks and blocks with that never ending lull of soft and gentle motion.

The 3 preschoolers were a different story. They were sometimes walking ... sometimes on a scooter ...

sometimes in a stroller. It was kind of a long trek for little preschooler legs but there was good motivation to keep on going ... the thrift store always has TOYS.

We spent about half an hour 'thrifting' and found treasures in the toy area. Brittany asked me if I had time to look for something for myself ... I don't even consider that an option when we are with the littles ... it is all about them and everyone was content as we began the hike home.

When we left the thrift store the two older children were on the scooters. Brittany had told me that two-year-old Taylor in the stroller, was good on a scooter too.

I could tell on the way home that the toddlers were wearing out. I was ready to get out of the sun and sit down for a while. I suggested that we take the shortcut across the grass on the backside of the housing development to get home.

The look on Brittany's face told me that it had never crossed her mind to take a cut-off. Her facial expression was almost like it would be cheating on a test at school, if you took a shortcut home.

The shortcut option apparently only got used by the rookie' babysitters like grandparents and uncles. Because Grandpa Joe and Uncle Robbie and me ... well we all knew how to take the shortcut and get home faster with worn out kids and adults.

Brittany said, "Let's stay on the sidewalk because the sidewalk is smooth for the scooter." I agreed . Good call! Two-year-old little Taylor was on a pink scooter ... even though she was a little petite for the scooter, she managed well.

It was like a merry-go-round stopping every 5 minutes with people switching seats. The kids all rotating between three modes of transportation; scooter - walking - stroller ... and then 5 minutes later they switch places again. The only consistent person was the six-week-old baby in a car seat in my stroller - otherwise the other three children were shifting constantly.

As we started down the sidewalk incline, I had to hang onto my baby stroller to keep it from running away downhill. The concrete was smooth, and the stroller needed no help going downhill, neither did the scooter need help going downhill. Soon I heard little Taylor on the scooter starting to cry! Scream actually!

She was coming down the hill ... on the concrete ... on the scooter ... she was balanced but completely out of control and had no way to STOP and she knew it!!

When I turned to look over my shoulder what I saw was complete terror in Taylors saucer-size eyes. Her face was red and her eyes were huge with fear and there was a scream just waiting to burst out of her mouth!!!

Behind Taylor, Brittany was still pushing her stroller. She hollered to me up front "Grandma STOP HER!!!!"

Over my shoulder I watched the out-of-control child and scooter speeding my way.   I had **one** chance ... only **one** chance ... and I knew it!

I was hanging onto my downhill rolling stroller with my right hand and with my left hand I reached out and ... caught the upright crossbar of the scooter solidly. Man, it was a beautiful thing! Not a wobble from the scooter ... Taylor never fell ... never got knocked over ... just a nice abrupt yet graceful stop ... it was an Olympic gold performance!

Safe from harm yet petrified with fear Taylor stepped off the scooter and screamed - and cried - and screamed - and cried as she climbed into the front seat of her mother's stroller.

Now the two older children got out of the stroller to walk.

I could hardly keep from busting out laughing as the merry-go-round of moving parts kept going around and around. Brittany in control of all of it.

The six-week-old baby was still asleep in my stroller ... Brittany was pushing the stroller with two scooters riding in a seat ... and a two-year-old in the **front still screaming**.

After we got down to level sidewalk, Taylor was still sobbing out the fear ... Brittany assured her that she did not get hurt ... Brittany said to little Taylor, "Maybe you should say, "Grandma thank you for stopping me.'"

With big gulps of air and sobs she gasped around her tears "grandma ...(gasp) thank you (gasp) ...for (gasp) ... stopping (gasp) ... me." Her sobbing began to subside, and everybody fell into a comfortable pace walking the last few blocks to the safety of home. I marveled and shook my head those last few minutes.

As we walked back home, I knew that every step for Brittany is a teaching moment. She is a master ... everyday ... every moment she it tutoring their children. I take her lead and when I am in charge, I try to do everything the way she does it! It never works for me the way it works for her!

Every intersection we approached she was teaching and coaching and guiding them ... which way to look ... where to go... she is actively loving them. We could have just stayed home but that would never be an option for this mom.

Brittany never takes the short cut when it comes to raising their children ... take the easy way? Heck no! There's' a lot at stake and she knows it. Absolutely everything she can teach them now, will save them having to learn it the hard way later in life.

I had a great time! It's not every day you get to be a hero ... I got to save the day and hear little Taylor's gasping voice say, "grandma ... thank you ...for ... stopping ... me."

 I also know that I will **never have this chance again** ... I had one shining moment today ... Taylor was scared – she learned from it – her mom coached her through it ... and she will not make that mistake again – and tomorrow 100% guaranteed ... without a doubt ... Taylor's going to get back on that scooter ... and she will never again need grandma to stop her.

I am grateful! I loved being Taylor's hero today ... I loved the feeling inside as I drove home ... but mostly I loved that Brittany let ME ... her mother in law ... trusted me enough to say, "Grandma STOP her!"... and she knew I would ... I loved being a part of Brittany's curriculum.

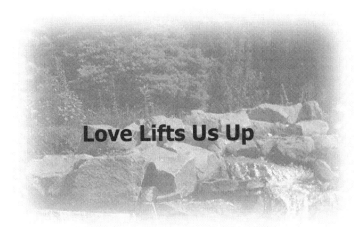

Love Lifts Us Up

I was the only one who saw it. Everybody else was ordering sandwiches at the counter while I was watching the toddler. The stranger standing in line at the sandwich shop was trying to get a smile out of her - that little 18-month-old granddaughter of mine. Little Miss Taylor had a ponytail on top of her head that splayed out like a miniature water fountain, bobbing from side to side with each step. With big saucer eyes she soberly stared at the man as if frozen by a spell. The man was exaggerating his grin and doing a finger-wiggle-wave, trying everything possible, in hopes of winning a smile. The 18-month-old had to make a decision about the man ... and she was not buying it. Her straight face said the guy was failing miserably.

And yet, just 10 minutes earlier, the same little girl, saw a big burly man on the sidewalk, that was not her daddy, and she ran to him with open abandon! What the heck!!!

It had all happened quickly and spontaneously, with four adults watching.

Just ten minutes earlier, my son Robbie and I had been standing on the sidewalk waiting for his younger brother Tom & family to arrive at the sandwich shop. The autumn temperatures were comfortable, so we waited at the corner on the sidewalk, with the steady sound of small-town traffic going by.

A few minutes later the family pulled up and parked. We watched as Tom and Brittany got out of the vehicle, helping their three little ones out of seatbelts and car seats and lifting them safely onto the walkway.

Everyone was watching the littlest munchkin, Taylor, get steady on her feet there on the sidewalk. When she noticed Grandma and uncle Robbie waiting to greet them, she got a BIG smile and started 'toddler-running' the short distance in our direction ... the little ponytail was bouncing double time from side to side, everyone watching the smiling little girl. With arms spread wide ...she ran as fast as her little legs could carry her ...she ran right past grandma into the open outstretched arms of ... big Uncle Robbie! With one solid swoop she was in his big safe arms, head gently nestled on his strong shoulder.

Like the winning touchdown at a Super Bowl, a ROAR went up from the family! The sports announcer in my head was saying, " WHAT_A_ PLAY!!! Did you see that folks !?! There has **never** been a play like this since the beginning of the sport! Little Miss Taylor executing a 'quarterback sneak' right past her grandma and the touchdown undecidedly goes to ... Uncle Robbie!!! " There it was ... a million-dollar hug.

All this took less than a minute to unfold. Robbie's intimidating size: his towering and broad physical presence, his bigness, his deep voice, and beard - all of it was gone. All that was left was ... love.

The stranger inside the restaurant was well-meaning but didn't have a chance. Because Little girl hugs don't come cheap. Trust doesn't come cheap. Robbie willingly earned it in a million different ways. He has held her since the day she arrived. Just days after she was born, she heard his voice talking to her in soothing tender tones. He watches over her safety with an eagle eye. His big hands willingly play with little girl purses and pretend lipstick. On the floor together she playfully pushes against the gentle giant, and he willingly yields to her shenanigans. His deep voice softens to read fairy tale stories one after another ... one moment at a time, adding warmth and playfulness and mixing it all together, creating complete Trust. It is not by chance that she runs to him ...

There are all kinds of currency in life. There's Money and Super Bowl trophies and Olympic gold medals ... and none of them could have bought that innocent ... spontaneous ... hug.   It's a knowing that goes deep inside her heart.

A knowing ... that great big Uncle Robbie's arms are not just going to catch her *today* ... but *will always* lift her up ... today and tomorrow and the tomorrow after tomorrow... lifting her up ... to bigger than she is right now ...

This Christmas ... wishing you... love that lifts you up...

Cathy and Joe

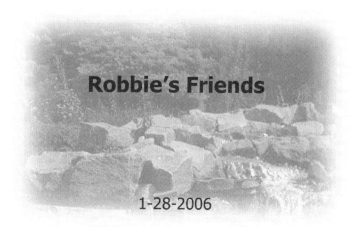

Robbie's Friends

1-28-2006

I highly doubt that I had a drink all night. Spending hours together in a bar with my son and his friends; talking about the BIG stuff called LIFE. I swear there is no conversation I'd rather have! Give me the **real** stuff. I'd rather think deeply and hear who you really are than any kind a facade ... I hate that. I drove home sober, satisfied and feeling filled up with great discussion with awesome young men.

Later that night when I called to tell Rob I was not joining them at the next bar for more life learning conversations ... he said, "Boy you should have heard the conversation in the car after you left! They said they'd have NEVER been able to have a conversation with one of their parents like that! No way!"

And then the kicker. He said "I'm so proud to have you as my mom. And I'd like to be able to say that I had something to do with it – but I didn't."

What a compliment!

But really, you did have a lot to do with it Rob.

On your own, without me, you created rock solid friendships with the people that you shared with me tonight. With open arms everyone welcomed me; because of you. I want to know who the person in front of me really is … who they are on the inside and how they got that way and that is especially true when it's YOU.

My love for **you** created in **me** a set of priorities and a drive so strong, that I want to understand who you are and to LISTEN to you so intently and a desire to connect so completely so there is a companionship of mind.

I'd rather take a deep dive any day … anytime … anywhere … just be real with me … that's all … me with you and you with me … show me your good stuff and your vulnerable place … because I have all of that too … and we will be best of friends … and I'm going to love everything about you … I promise.

LuLu
10 31 2017

"She has the cancer".

That's exactly how she said it to me. My 13-year-old granddaughter Maggie, telling me about Lulu, the smallest cuddliest non-assuming dog that ever walked the earth. You could find her on a doggie bed, not making any kind of a fuss. Maybe because she was so little, she tried hard to stay out of the way. In the past, LuLu had bouts of not eating or drinking and up until now, the vet always worked his magic and found a way to help her. Little Miss Lulu slept each night in bed by Maggie's side.

As LuLu progressively became more frail, there eventually came the morning with the emotional turmoil. Maggie awoke and thought LuLu had died. The steady decline and the awareness that their daughter may only remember LuLu in this state, prompted a family meeting to decide what to do next and what the options were.

Good advice came from the experts on the internet. The experts said to 1) Call for an appointment ahead of time to have the animal euthanized. 2) Pay for it right away so that afterwards - after it's over you can leave and not have to talk to anyone.

Lu Lu's blanket was one of the many I had personalized with my embroidery machine for my grandson through the years. Sometimes LuLu slept on top of it all curled up in a ball and I had also seen it being used as a covering for the cage LuLu sometimes slept in at night to create a sense of soft comfort all around her.

The night before LuLu was euthanized, John sat watching football with Lulu on his chest - knowing that time was running out. Even as he sat holding her, he started making the arrangements that were inevitable. He knew that he could not do this alone. He began by calling one of those friends who would do anything for you. Chris answered the call and scheduled the appointment for the next day, even offering to do the task himself. As John felt LuLu breathing in and out on his chest, John knew that was not an option.

The next day Chris did the driving, and the two friends went together with LuLu. A designated special room at the vet clinic was designed for crossing over. LuLu died in the blanket I had embroidered and would be cremated with it as well – that made me happy to know she was comfortably wrapped in my love too. This space is uninterrupted afterwards, allowing humans to take all the time they need to say goodbye without hurrying.

As they left the clinic with empty arms, two big men with puddles of tears – already missing a 3-pound dog and wondering how a tiny little body like that can demand and obtain so much love?

Stepping out into the warm Arizona sun, Chris dropped the tailgate of his truck and offered John a seat. He opened a cooler ... took out a bottle of scotch, ice cubes and two glasses. It was time to honor Little Miss LuLu.

I love that a three-pound dog can bring out the love in two great big highly motived men ... asking them to stop in their tracks to spend a little time ...honoring a life that could so easily have gone unnoticed ...

Together they toasted ... together they talked and cried unapologetically ... letting LuLu be the center of attention on this important day ... this was tailgating at its finest ... cheers to you LuLu!!!!

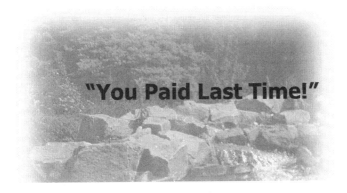

"You Paid Last Time!"

"You paid last time, it's my turn!" said the elderly woman in the stylish red coat.

Perkins was busy and Robbie was patiently waiting to buy cookies.

Robbie – he's one of those people who connects with people no matter where he goes... even at Perkins.

The two ladies in front of him were playfully arguing over who gets to pay for lunch. He smiled at the polite sparring going on between the two women because he loves those good-natured friendship type arguments.

As the one woman was paying for lunch the other one said, "OK I'll get the car then."

The counter assistant asked if they could help Robbie, but he said he was just there for baked goods. The woman in the stylish red coat turned around and apologized.
"Sorry I'm holding you up!"

As she paid her bill and was putting the wallet back in her purse Robbie told her there was no rush at all ... putting her keys and phone and wallet away ... putting on gloves and hat and bundling herself up for the cold temperatures.

Finally, the woman behind the counter asked Robbie what he wanted. This prompted the woman in the red coat to apologize one more time.

Politely Robbie asked for a dozen chocolate chip cookies ... at this the woman in the red coat whirled around with a huge smile on her face and said; "One is for me right?"

Without missing a beat Robbie said "Of course!"

And they both laughed.

The server had to go in the back to get more cookies to complete the order. Robbie turned around and the red coat was gone. A feeling of disappointment flashed through him as he was feeling a little bummed about not giving her a cookie. A minute later he paid and had a full bag of cookies in hand as he stepped outside ... thinking maybe he could catch her. But she was nowhere to be seen.

As he walked to his vehicle he looked over his shoulder just one more time and sure enough he saw a red coat in the passenger seat of a jeep. With a smile on his face, Rob stepped into the middle of the parking lot; bag of cookies raised above his head. All the while he was pointing at the parking spot next to his vehicle.

He could see the woman in red coat directing the driver to pull over ... the women came toward Rob with huge smiles on their face while the woman in red rolled her window down.

Rob took two cookies from the bag and said, "One for each of you. I love the color of your coat! Merry Christmas!"

They both laughed and thanked and spread merry Christmases all between the three of them before they went on their way.

I doubt that Robbie told anyone besides me about the cookies ... I'm sure it only came up in conversation between the two of us during one of those walk/talk times of getting some exercise ... and I'm sure he didn't guess that there would be a story written someday.

I have to wonder how much those two cookies cost? And what kind of return on investment did Robbie get? ... it was just for the fun of it all! But those cookies doubled and tripled in value for those ladies with each telling of the story ... the perfect way to end an already obviously wonderful time between two friends ... and then there's the retelling of the story; the woman in red retelling about asking for a cookie in a teasing way and retelling about being stopped in the parking lot. All of it adding up to a delicious little story ... with a sweet cookie at the end ... and each retelling increasing the value of those cookies.

And the dividend payment: I bet that each time they go to Perkins ... they remember again ... the young man who took the time to pay attention ... not for any other reason than ... just for the fun of it all.

The Most Beautiful Blanket in the World

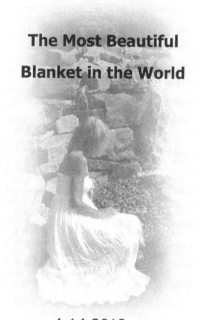

4-14-2018

Brady's 21st Birthday

It had already been repaired and re-covered once when it belonged to my firstborn son. The first time I bought new fabric to cover John's baby blanket was stressful. As I worked on the blanket, he watched every move I made … every stitch was under his watchful eye as he sat in the chair near the sewing machine – scrutinizing each little stitch … making sure that the blanket – the beautiful blanket … the one filled with comfort and love – THAT blanket was *really* inside the new fabric.

This spectacularly beautiful blanket originally had white soft fur on one side with a white bubble design on the other side with shimmering threads running through it. The edges of the blanket were encased with satin binding and on top of the binding, to hide the stitching, was a white brocade cording all the way around. This elegant beautiful baby blanket had now become his constant companion.

We let John use the beautiful blanket as his Grandmother Vera Weber had encouraged us to do. It was so beautiful I was tempted to display it over the edge of the crib and not use it at all.

As the years went by, it was losing its luster and the sparkle was gone. It had been dragged miles across floors and chewed on during teething. It was being used in the way his grandmother had intended – drooled on and cried on.

*****

Well *that* son grew up ... and he grew and he grew and he grew ... until he became a father himself. And the well-used re-covered blanket got passed on to his son Brady. That ratty old, hauled-through-the-dirt-blanket that was so soft and loved and it felt just right.

Little Brady used that dilapidated blanket and even took it with him as he and his parents moved to the desert heat of Arizona. The blanket kept the chill of air conditioning away at night and the little boy stayed warm and cozy.

The most beautiful blanket in the world became more tattered and torn as it was dragged across more floors and washed more times. Finally, at the age of 5 the little grandboy allowed me to put a new cover on the blanket.

Brady watched every move I made ... every stitch was under his watchful eye as he sat in the chair near the sewing machine – scrutinizing each little stitch ... making sure that the blanket – the most beautiful blanket ... the one filled with comfort and love – THAT blanket was *really* inside the new fabric. He watched my every move until the blanket was done.

*****

16 years later the blanket is tattered and torn once again. He himself, Brady, the grown-up grandson who has used it as a pillow beneath his head for 20 years, asks me to take it home to Minnesota – on an airplane, to put a new cover on the blanket once again.

Wow! he trusts me now; he doesn't need to watch me; he knows the old trusty blanket will be inside with a new cover. I placed it in my suitcase with reverence, knowing that I had been given something irreplaceable ... somehow it had become a treasure.

The blanket and I arrived safely in Minnesota. I went to work first washing it in a GENTLE cycle inside a laundry bag designed for delicate items.

When it was washed, I gingerly laid out the tattered blanket with torn edges. Strips of fabric were attached only by a thread or two that were delicately laid flat to dry in place. There were places where the original blanket peeked out ... reminding me of all those years ago, when John was born. The old fabric didn't seem to mind my tears.

I let it dry from the washer and from my tears; laying flat that way, as my mind figured out the process of gently putting the pieces back together. Working on the inside of the blanket first, I was getting all of the tattered pieces stitched in place for comfort.

At the fabric store I was serious and focused, looking for the exact right color and style of fabric. I found the orange basketball hoops on a black background - the perfect touch for the third time to re-cover this blanket that had now become a friend.

As I put layers back in place, I walked through the memories of my son's birth ... I walked through the joy of being present for HIS son's birth ... and I strolled through all of the in-betweens ... the life that unfolded in the long stretches of time in-between the blanket's recovering's.

That's where the most beautiful blanket in the world gets it's fame from ... from all those in-between times of going unnoticed ... just being there, available and ready ... patient and steadfast   ... elegantly flowing through life.

The first time I re-covered the most beautiful blanket in the world my son watched me like an eagle ...

The second time I re-covered the most beautiful blanket in the world, my grandson watched me like a hawk ...

The third time I re-covered the most beautiful blanket in the world my grandson asked me to take it home ... on an airplane ... and send it back to him.

One more time the blanket had been filled with my love ... stitch after stitch. I know the blanket was there at times, when I wished my arms could have taken its place ...

being there for the hard times, the good times, and the common everyday ordinary times.

After a waterfall of grateful tears, I took the final stitch ... gently packed the box ... and shipped the most beautiful blanket in the world ... back to Brady in Arizona ... for a new beginning.

It arrived ... on Brady's 21st birthday.

Red Firebird

June 13, 2019

The red firebird was shining so brightly you could hardly look at it in the early afternoon sun! The glare was magnificent! It was a photo shoot day ... just my son and I together. I invited him to the country that day to take photos of him in his car. I say that as if I were a professional photographer ... as if I really knew what I was doing. I was excited to take the photos.

Underneath the success of owning that red car is a man who struggled with alcohol for a time - got himself into trouble for a while – then got himself out of trouble – and then there came a tipping point - when continuing the old way was so heavy and dark, the perceived benefits of continuing the old way, was no longer an option.

Once his decision was made, everybody, and I mean everybody, came together to support his conviction. If you are one of those inner circle people and you are reading this story – you're feeling a chill down your spine right now, because you were in the trenches with Rob every step of the way, shoveling dirt out of that trench when needed.

I know because I've been there in the trenches too. At the bottom of a pit so deep, that the only option is to go up – because you can't get any lower. There **isn't** a level lower. Hopefully every person gets this gift of being at the bottom and lives to tell about it ... about that place that is so miserably awful you think the sheer pain of it will kill you ... but it doesn't ... the only thing that will kill you ... is giving up ... then you are laying in the trenches by yourself, not seeing the magnificent opportunity that is hidden inside the misery.

From this place of suffering, I told Rob "Someday you're going to realize this DUI is the best thing that ever happened to you." He looked at me wide-eyed, like I had just unexpectedly spoken a foreign language. He kept on shoveling ... day after day ... riding a bike in 30 below temperatures to work ... paying back what he owed ... getting back on top.

Then THAT day came ... yep ... the one when he realized that the DUI was the best thing that ever happened to him. He was doing something simple ... just eating a doughnut ... in complete freedom. Not owing anybody anymore. He had become free. It came with deep struggle ... but that deep struggle had rendered him ... FREE.

As he took that final step out of the trench, the world of possibility opened before him.

He bought the red firebird.

Like a mountain climber sticking a flag at the summit – the bright red car was saying "I'm back! I'm here! I made it out of the pit to the top of the mountain. I can look around from up here and see so much more clearly."

So today was photo shoot day – just me and my son – in the country with wide open space ... a red firebird gleaming in the sunshine – and the pride of a mother, capturing her son's feeling of success.

I took my time editing those photos ... turning them to Black and White ... leaving only the car bright red. It was stunning! So stunning that the employee at the photo counter would NOT give me the pictures. The employee wanted the copyright release from the photographer.

I opened my phone to the photo gallery to show proof that I had indeed taken these photos. The employee was shocked and quietly gave me my photographs.

The employee thought it was the photographer that made those pictures magnificent ... but I know better ... it was PRIDE that made those photos so glorious. Pride emanating from my son ... spreading pride inside that car ... he had done IT ... overcome that obstacle deep inside ... that thing that keeps us from being our very BEST self ... yes THAT obstacle; he had conquered it.

The car knew it ...

Rob knew it ... even the camera knew it ... it was PRIDE.

Mr. Swanson 12 15 2020 by John M. Weber

3:22 ... LTE

< Notes

December 15, 2020 at 4:45 PM

Swanson

Note: student name changed for privacy

Last year I took Maggie to deliver a care package to a special needs classmate between Christmas and New Years. I wasn't sure what to expect but Maggie wanted to make sure do something nice for this young man, while he was recovering from an extended hospital stay in a medical rehab/transition facility. When we arrived we were greeted by Maggie's Unified Teacher, Mr Swanson. I had heard much about this man and had a mental picture of a man that was much different than the one who greeted us. Mr Swanson is tallish and you can tell an athlete at some point in his life. He shook my hand and we immediately hit it off. We talked business, life and sports while we waited to see Max and deliver the basket. My first impression of Mr. Swanson was, "this is a man's man". What happened next I was not prepared for. We walked into Max's room and in the bed was a mid-teen age boy who's body had shriveled to about 60-70 pounds. He had lost his sight in the last year and couldn't hear very well. He was unaware that we had entered the room. Of course Mr. Swanson knew this and walked softly to the side of the bed. He knelt down and softly touched Max's arm which startled him a bit but then Max moved his hand to Swansons. Then Swanson leaned right next to Max's ear and talked to him for at least 10 minutes. I recall the striking level of compassion that this man had at the time. He told Max how much he loves him. Told him about class and that the kids miss him. Then he had Maggie come over and take his place. She spoke with Max a bit and once Max got tired, we left the basket behind and walked out with Swanson. I spoke with him a bit afterwards and was amazed at the many layers of this man.

Fast forward to today. Nearly a year later, Christmas is 9 days away. We got the news that Max had passed away. Mr Swanson delivered the news and said he had been there just hours before Max passed and had whispered in Max's ear how much he is loved. I have no doubt it was in the same tender caring manner that I had the privilege to witness. Today is certainly a sad day for Max and his family. I can only imagine how many times over the last year that Swanson sat next to that bed and talked to the young man. A young man that he has been caring for as a teacher for many years. When they first met, Max could see and hear and was always making others smile. His autoimmune disease slowly took those things from him but it never took Mr. Swanson love.

So today, in what might be the crappiest year on record, I hope you know there are heroes that walk among us. There may never be a parade in his honor but if you know Nick Swanson, give him a hug for me.

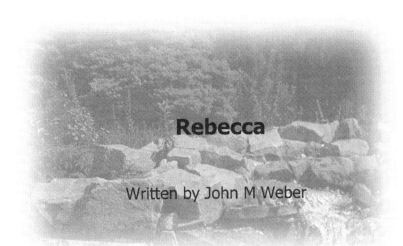

Rebecca

Written by John M Weber

June 13th, 2021, around 11 am, Shannon and I pull up to the QT to get something quick. As I pull in to park, I notice a young woman sitting around the side of the building in the shade. It was already about 100 degrees, and she was sipping on some water. She appeared to be thinking about her life and possibly how she ended up at a QT off 99th and Camelback on a Sunday morning. She looked like she wanted to cry but was holding it together. I went into the store to get the items we needed. As I walked past her, she didn't look up or say anything. I figured she would ask for money, but she didn't, she just stared off into the distance. As I came back from the store, I walked past her again and it was the same, no eye contact, no saying hi or asking for money. I got back in the truck and looked at Shannon as I was putting my seatbelt on and I said "So, what do we do here?". She shrugged and said, "I don't know, what can we do?". Having a 24-year-old son in recovery for addiction, we know all too well that giving her money is not an option but something in my gut told me I needed to go talk to her. I took off my seatbelt and told Shannon I would go chat with her. As I approached her, she looked up at me with a scared and intimidated look on her face. I calmly knelt down a few feet away from her to get on her level and show her that I meant no harm. I asked her what she was doing out here and she said she was waiting.

I asked for what and she said she didn't know. She explained that she had been with a man yesterday and this morning he kicked her out with no ability to get back home. She didn't have a cell phone but asked if she could use mine. I asked her who she would call and she said she would call her in mom in California who would figure out a way to get her home. Her home is in Maricopa (a small city about an hour away). I asked how old she was, she said 33. I said, ok, I'm going to talk to my wife. I go back over to the truck and Shannon rolls her window down. I explained the situation and told her, that we have to figure out a way to get her back to Maricopa. As parents of an addict, we know the sinking feeling of getting a call from your child in distress and wanted to help if we could. Shannon suggest that we order her an Uber to take her home, an idea that hadn't occurred to me yet as I was thinking through the options with my connections. We both returned to chat with Rebecca. She agreed to take an Uber and gave me her address in Maricopa. I ordered the uber and we walked around to the other side of the gas station where the Uber would pick her up. The app alerted me that the driver was 7 minutes away. I knew I had 7 minutes to figure out what more we could do to help. Shannon went inside to get us all some water. I told Rebecca at that time that we have a 24-year-old son who is in recovery from drug addiction and the we feel that if we can help others, then the universe will in turn help our son.

She started to cry and told me that she knew what Brady is going through. She said that she is an addict and regularly used Meth and pills. I asked what kind of pills, and she said fentanyl. An answer that I'm sure she expected to be judged for. I just looked and nodded and asked her if she had ever been to rehab. She said she had detoxed once but didn't go to rehab. I asked if she had heard of Unhooked Recovery, and she said had called there once but the wait list was too long so she didn't go. I told her that we have a connection there through our friends, Kim Peacock and Cory Flotta who have a foundation that provides scholarships for people battling addiction for both rehab and sober living. I asked if she would be open to going to rehab if we could use our connections to get her a bed quickly. She cried again and said she would. At this point, Shannon was back with our waters and in tears herself. We asked how we contact her and she gave us her mom's name and number. She said her mom would know how to get in touch with her. Shannon offered her a hug and she declined, stating that she was dirty and sweaty. The uber showed up, I opened the back door for her and she got in and gave us a little smile and a "thank you". I tapped on the drivers window, he rolled it down and I bent over to look him in the eyes and I said "take good care of this young woman". No more words were necessary, he knew I meant business.

We watched the Uber leave and I tracked her ride on the app, she was delivered to her house in Maricopa safely about an hour later. In the time between the Uber picking her up and getting her home, we contacted Kim/Cory, shared the story and asked for their help. Without hesitation, Kim was on it. She called Diane (Rebecca's mom) and told her that her daughter was safe and that we had put her in an uber. Diane was driving from CA to AZ because she hadn't heard from Rebecca in a few days and was worried. I can only imagine the relief she must have felt getting that call from a stranger. Kim asked Diane if she could work on getting Rebecca a bed at Unhooked Recovery. Diane agreed and the wheels were set in motion. Kim made the call to Unhooked where she knows many of the people who run that facility.

She found there was a resident checking out yesterday and they would indeed have a bed in the women's facility for Rebecca. Given their long wait list, this is a miracle. Kim called Diane to let her know the good news and Diane said that she had just arrived in AZ and that Rebecca was going to shower, pack a bag and they would be taking her to rehab that night. You can imagine the emotions that Shannon and I felt as we were getting updates from Kim every hour or two. Later that evening around 7 pm came **the text we had been waiting for**, Rebecca had been checked into rehab at Unhooked Recovery.

Shannon connected with Diane via text to let her know we are here if she needs anything. She was very grateful for what we had done and offered to pay for the Uber ride. Of course, we declined but asked that she find a way to pay it forward one day. We hope to stay in touch with Diane and hear about Rebecca's progress.

**My personal note: I cannot even imagine the mother that was gifted her child back – not dead on a stretcher-- but being retuned in an Uber ... by two people using their Time ... their Money ... and Connections to save a life ...

the life of someone who was sitting on a sidewalk at a Quik Trip.

If I were that mother, I would set aside time every single day... for the rest of my life ... a time to give thanks for the MIRACLE that was bestowed upon ... a mother and her child.

Legacy Plants

I've never told anyone about my mother's plant. You see my mom passed back in 2001. I had a plant of hers and after her passing it was looking DISMAL. Pretty much the plant looked like I FELT ... dad and mom died within three months of each other, and it knocked the wind out of my sails, to say the least.

Back in 2001 with plant in hand and deep in grief, I went to my neighbor, Richard, to ask if he thought the plant would survive. Richard was a country hermit, who had worked his career at the arboretum at the University of Minnesota. He was my best source of advice. As Richard looked at the plant, he did not want to give me false hope. He said, "It MIGHT make it."

I pampered the plant, and it began to grow. Weeks later, I noticed there was an offspring coming up from the soil! I very carefully took the new volunteer plant – separating the roots – and planting the offspring in its own little pot. Then I had two! With each new plant I assured myself that even if one died, I would still have another.

It was at this point, twenty years ago, that I made a vow. Every offspring from this plant was going to be rooted and planted and shared with others. In my mind I called it a 'legacy plant'. Years went by and no one knew why I had so many extra plants and offered them to everyone. I can't even begin to count how many plants have been gifted to others through the course of 20 years... Sometimes I take them to nursing homes or elder care facilities, sometimes to offices ...

When Joe's dad passed, years later, we inherited a plant from him ... and in his memory I made the same commitment. There are times I am in an office downtown and I see a 'legacy plant' and I just smile thinking about the destiny of each one. A part of my parent's life and a part of Joe's parent's life continuing ... in a quiet beautiful way.

Earlier this summer I set a bench at the end of my driveway with 8 potted plants and within three hours they all had new homes. This time, they are sitting in the sun at Living Tree Massage/The Grove.

I buy pots at garage sales and in clearance aisles and keep them in a cupboard in my garage. Joe built a potting counter for me and he brings in finely ground gopher dirt and puts it in buckets and totes in my garage for planting in the winter time. Winter is the hardest because I can't take them out in the cold to disperse them, so usually by spring there are many waiting for new homes.

This story is getting long ... and I don't know why NOW is the time to tell it ... maybe... because after 20 years... I still miss them.

The plants:

They get watered once a week on Sunday morning.

They are in real soil, so they are heavy.

They have been loved and nurtured and passed on by me ... in loving memory of Joe's dad ... and my mom.

Pity Party

I was the only person invited to the Coronavirus Pity Party ... well, maybe not.

I'm sure I wasn't the only one that wanted my life and my freedom back. I wanted to freely see my grandchildren and to play.

I purchased a couple of kid's tin lunch boxes for Cameron and Tatum with little kid handles on them and a latch just like an old-fashioned lunch boxes I saw when I was a little girl. Cameron's was decorated with Mickey and Minnie mouse and Tatum's was decorated with the characters from the movie Frozen. I had a fabulous time picking out little toys to put inside the lunchboxes ... knowing that each one of them would love carrying them around!

I bought dominoes to put in Tatum's box and I bought some game pieces to put in Cameron's box. 57 pieces to be exact! Cameron loves to play with frying pans, both big and small ones, and I knew that he would be putting these pieces in his frying pan and pretending to stir food and cook with them. So, at the same time I bought him a set of kitchen tongs - the ones that have heat resistant hands on the end – yes hands in the shape of people's hands.

Those little lunch boxes were sitting in an out of the way place. Each time I looked at them I would feel sorry for myself, because I wanted to give them to Cameron and Tatum myself. I wanted to BE with them and watch them play with them … I wanted to have it all.

A couple of days later after I had filled the lunch boxes until they would hold no more … they were put together and completed, I was once again in a Pity Party. I was about to leave the house and go to the post office, to mail a book to a friend who lives across town. I could've easily dropped it off at her home but because of Coronavirus I put it in an envelope and mailed it to her.

It was this day that I was heading to the post office when I looked at those lunchboxes again and finally chastised myself and said, "Get over the pity party and just send them in the mail."

So, I put them in a box and sent them to Fargo … the next night when I was talking with the kids on Facetime the parents said that the kids were going stir crazy! There was no place to go and nothing to do! I told them that this was a really good time to get some new toys.

The next day the package arrived, and I received 13 pictures of those two little peanuts opening and playing with their presents!!!! And later in the evening I received a video of little Cameron still up at about 8:30 PM … playing with those new toys. Sigh … big deep breath of contentment.

Once I got over my pity party and started thinking about someone else – thinking about my grandchildren instead of *feeling sorry for myself* ... then *my heart could get filled up beyond words*.

Once I left the Pity Party, I received JOY in abundance. Two little children receiving a gift during a difficult time. I received the JOY of those parents having a diversion and taking a break from a global pandemic ... it had come in the mail from grandma ... it was love in a box ... and I had learned ... to leave the pity party ... sooner than later.

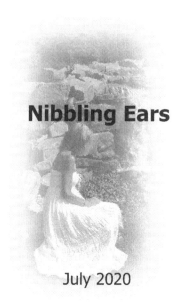

Nibbling Ears

July 2020

"Nibble ears grandma!!" the children begged.

My son looked at me and asked "What is that?"

It all started so innocently, one day kissing Cameron's face while I tucked him in for naptime, and I gently nuzzled and nibbled on the top of his ear ... the sensation made him stop and sit quietly. So, I did it again the next time in the quiet minutes before sleep.

When Mom says it's naptime Tatum tries hard to delay the moment and says, "Grandma sing songs and nibble ears!" I lay on the soft carpet between their beds to sing. In the darkened room little Tatum's hand will flop out between the bars of the crib and as we sing, I rub the soft skin on the back of her hand that is dangling there. When they have had enough singing one of them will say, "Nibble ears now" and then my lips gently nuzzle, nibble, and kiss the tops of their ears ... kisses down the side of the face, onto the neck, breathing warm against their face ... the softness of their skin and "I love you's" whispered up and down each side; sometimes the words are whispered so close to their ear that it tickles ... sometimes not whispered at all, just thought without words.

I start with Cameron, the oldest because ... well, because he was there first. His ears are easily accessible now that he is in a big boy's bed. No more curving over the side of his crib, trying to nibble the ear tops. When Cam is saturated with nibbles and kisses, I move just a few feet away to Tatum's crib.

Leaning over the side of the crib I feel like a twisted pretzel or a bent coat hanger trying to reach her ears. While in this bent over position, I feel my cell phone being expertly lifted out from my back pocket ... Cameron, that little turkey, there in the dark.

As I finish soundlessly nibbling Tatum's ears, she drifts off to sleep. When I stand up and turn around, Cameron gives the phone back to me and in the shadow of the nightlight I see his huge grin. Those brown eyes sparkling! With Tatum already sleeping and Cameron, the pickpocket, quieted now, I am tiptoeing from the darkened room, when a wee small voice quietly whispers from the darkness " I love you".

I leave the room with tears in my eyes and a scrunched up face that is trying to not let the tears fall. More than once my daughter-in-law has seen me leaving a quiet nap room weeping. She knows they said something priceless, and I try to tell her but the words won't come.

I look at Brittany and I remember what it was like having three little ones under the age of four myself. There is no feeling sorry for her -- all the work - all the non-stop activity ... she is exactly where she wants to be ... and so was I – I loved every moment. Deep in the trenches of teaching, directing, guiding, and watching her children ... watching for the qualities she knows they will need ...

She knows in the future they will need each other for love and support. One day Tatum got pushed down by a neighbor boy when they were playing outside. When she tried to get up the little boy pushed her down again. This time Cameron came to defend his little sister for the very first time.

How do I know this happened for the first time on June 13th, 2020? Because my daughter in law told me when it happened. She had been waiting for the day ... when her firstborn son would defend his smaller sister, for the very first time.

I wrote it down because there will be a day for my sweet son & his wife, when THEIR children will be grown up 'way too fast' and they will wonder 'where did all of those tiny little moments go?' 'Where is the sound of little morning feet pattering on the floor to the breakfast table?'

For now, the young parents are happily exhausted falling into bed each night and they won't remember what day and date that Cameron first defended his sister ... but I will remember for them, bringing them little bits of love in a story that will come in handy later for them and for me. Every tidbit adds to the story ... nibbling ears has become a story ... and that story became the story of Cameron loving and protecting his sister ... and each little love is attached to another little love ... it all starts so innocently, until there is a bond called 'Family' ... the pieces fit together so innocently ... held together by the glue of tiny moments of love ... like protecting your sister ... and nibbling ears.

PILLOW TIME

8 28 2022

It was a 3AM feeding and Joe got up with me the first night; now on the third night of feeding Grandbaby Lexi, I comfort the baby with her bottle by myself, in the quiet of the soft night lights. I don't mind ... as a matter of fact I treasure it.

It makes me remember when I thought the middle of the night thing was going to last forever – those night feedings, when my babies were small, and I couldn't wait until the baby sleeps through the night ... all too soon it was gone and I had moved on to the next stage without noticing – until now as a grandma, holding baby in the middle of the night ... I see it all so differently. Now I thank God there is enough milk ... I thank God there is enough breath ... I thank God for LIFE.

I went back to bed.

Later that night Taylor woke me screaming. I was ready to take her to the bathroom, but all she wanted was her pillow – that softness to sleep on that was two inches away from her head. That's all she wanted. I laid her on the pillow and now she was content and quiet, as I padded back to the bedroom that belongs to my son and his wife.

I quietly slip back into bed next to my husband. We both know we are only holding space for the real parents – there is no deception here ... we haven't built the relationship that this house of love is built on ... we are simply caring for it ... keeping the walls and the floors and the ceiling in place, while the owners are away.

Thank God Joe and I can pretend that we are important ... we can pretend that we are helping out; yet we have no idea how their parents have done all this heavy lifting ... and they make it look easy ... keeping them on schedule ... feeding on time ... bottles and snacks ... outside play time laughing with neighborhood children ... all of it culminating at the end of the day. We are struggling to get everyone showered and bathed before bed ... They spend time on their Kindles winding down from a nonstop day and I am sure they are sleeping within minutes of tumbling into bed.

As Joe and I get into bed ... we are smiling and so sleepy there is no time to count sheep. The days have been filled with love in motion – that nonstop movement of little legs and arms and excitement about exploring anything new ... new weeds along a sidewalk ... new kids to play side by side with at the park ... a new bug.

Then there is the nighttime ... that middle of the night feeling that gives pause ... a place to reflect ... when a newborn baby lays sweetly and innocently in my arms and it all feels so good ... life is quiet then and easier than one would think ... and I see things that were impossible to recognize when I was younger ... I might have missed it a couple of decades ago.

 Now I appreciate my eyes and my perspective as I see a moment ... when just moving the pillow ... two inches to the right ... under the tiny head of a toddler ... makes everything right with the world.

"Of Course!"

"Of course!" was the response to my text message. My son said it was OK to Facetime three little kiddos who just happen to be our grandchildren.

One weekend we had the grandchildren here at our farm when there were just barely three. The littlest one being just a six-week-old peanut for sure.

The entire weekend I would ask Cameron questions just to hear his response. I couldn't help it; it was so darn cute!

"Of course!" he said like his daddy. Although it sounded more like "a course", to nearly every question I asked ... he answered, 'a course'. I knew he was saying it because he hears his daddy say it to his requests. He sounded so adult that I spent the weekend asking unnecessary questions just to hear him say it.

I remember a little boy in daycare years ago named Chase. Chase had a unique characteristic as he was growing through toddlerhood. He talked in a sing song manner – his voice flowing up and down all the time, even though he was talking and not singing. I honestly don't even know how to describe it, I have never heard another child do it ... not ever, in 27 years of daycare was there another child with this unique characteristic. I told Chase's mom she needed to record it, but I don't think she ever did ... and neither did I record the 'a course'. I thought for sure I had time!!!! I thought for sure he'd say it again ... but he hasn't. It was just that one weekend ...

Maybe someday I will hear those words from little Cameron again ... and maybe not ... and maybe it wasn't meant to be recorded, maybe just meant to be enjoyed ... Joe and I and Rob remember it – we have talked about how dang cute it was ... and maybe that's enough.

Pheasant for Lunch

Pheasant for Dinner

12 19 2018

A BEAUTIFUL bird – a pheasant – was dead near the center line of the county road at the end of our driveway. I arrived home about noon that day ... and I could see as I drove by the roadkill that the fleshy part of the bird, the breast, was not badly damaged. This is only something a country girl would look for. Nobody else would care, but I had a good reason to care.

I put my car away in the garage, greeted the dog and grabbed a plastic shovel. With the shovel over my shoulder, I headed down the driveway like Davey Crockett on foot with our gorgeous shepherd husky, Tate, curiously prancing behind me. He hadn't noticed the roadkill yet and was following about 15 paces behind me.

Tate stayed back from the road while I got close to the bird. I slid the blade of the shovel underneath the pheasant and carried it up the driveway into our front yard. With each step up the driveway Tate followed closer and was sniffing the air all around the shovel. He came curiously close as I laid the still warm bird down in the front yard.

I waited and watched the dog's response. Tate was sniffing all around the bird. The pheasant must have passed the scent test because he gingerly took the bird in his mouth, moved to an out of the way place in the shade on the grass, and he began having pheasant for lunch.

While he was distracted and eating his lunch, I took the same shovel and picked up deer bones that he had hauled into the yard from the fields where the hunters had dumped bones, leaving them to be hauled away by wild coyotes. Tate had claimed and hauled some of the bones back into our yard and they had been gnawed clean and left scattered around the yard, ready for the garbage. It felt good to have the yard looking somewhat clean – not like an animal graveyard.

With the old deer bones cleaned up and Tate contentedly eating fresh pheasant for lunch, I finally came into the house leaving the dog to enjoy the great outdoors. 20 minutes later I looked out the window and saw ... to my surprise ... MORE fresh deer bones laying in the yard ... sigh ... the carcass and feathers from the pheasant scattered everywhere ... sigh ... what can I say? He lives by instinct ... I give up!

This day Tate won the prize ... fresh pheasant for lunch ... fresh deer bones for dessert. I should have served it with a glass of champagne!

Pheasant Part 2

The big windows in the front entry face the sunset. In the summertime those big windows get washed and squeegeed four or five times a year. In the country that is a recipe for unintentional bird self-annihilation. The birds see the sky's reflection in the glass, it appears that there is wide open flying space in front of them ... and they crash and burn.

Sometimes the bird is just stunned and they eventually get back up and fly away. Other times they hit so hard that they break their neck and fall to the ground dead.

One day as I was doing laundry, I heard a great big solid WHOMP! on the window. It felt like the house shook. I was shocked! I ran to the front of the house wondering if the window had broken. I looked out and saw that a pheasant had hit the glass, broken its neck and fell to the ground. I could see an imprint of dust and small feathers on the glass from the impact, as I gawked at the dead foul right there in front of me.

Outside in the yard I saw the startled look on Joe's face as he heard the hit all the way across the yard! He looked at the house wondering what in the world the big bang was!

From another location in the yard, I saw our dog Tate abruptly look up too, as he heard the hit!

A pheasant lay dead on the ground.

Simultaneously, my husband and the dog both started running from two separate directions ... racing to be the first one to get to the prized pheasant. It was like a movie in slow motion one frame at a time.

As I watched from the window, I was laughing myself silly! Joe knew if the dog got it first, he could out-run and out-hide and out-smart us for sure! The only hope of keeping that pheasant for us was to get to it first.

A dog and a man ... there should have been a sports commentator calling each stride ... neck and neck ... one human ... one dog ... ready to dive to the finish line.

With arms outstretched Joe grabbed the bird, pushing aside the dog. The game was over almost as soon as it had begun ... Tate sulked away ... looking as if he had somehow been cheated. Like a Superbowl trophy the pheasant was laid on top of a fence post, out of Tate's reach until it could be cleaned.

I wanted to remind Tate that **last time** there was a pheasant, I had delivered it to the front yard for him for lunch ... but the dog was **not** taking the loss well ... he was used to winning ... the land we live on has become his personal hunting domain and using his hunting instincts keeps him supplied with his heart's desire ... except for this one time ... this one instance when man vs animal and our smart, beautiful dog got left in the dust.

This time: Joe was faster, stronger, and smarter. The feast had been delivered right to our front window and we were going to enjoy it! The cleaned fresh bird was put in the crock pot with a cream sauce ... letting the aroma fill the house ... served on a bed of wild rice ...

Now it was our turn ... oh yes, it was fine! ...   pheasant for dinner ...

... and yes ... Joe and I ... **did** have champagne!

OREO

I stepped off the plane in Mesa and wheeled my suitcase into the waiting area. I heard my granddaughter's voice from a distance, "Grandma!" as she ran across the room. I held her in my arms for a really long time, and said, "Facetime is great, but it feels so much better to hold you in my arms!" John and Shannon were going to be hiking the Grand Canyon, leaving Maggie and I to spend a few days hanging out together.

<u>Five months ago</u>, one day in June, Maggie called on Facetime ... showing me a dog ... a dog in despair ... a depleted dog that had been wandering for months through alleys looking for food...a deteriorating body... matted twisted fur ... exhausted. He had obviously been lost and drifting in the Arizona heat. I could see the worry on Maggie's face as she held the dog in one arm and the phone with the other.

She told me her dad had seen a dog running along the side of the road. There was a truck that had pulled over and her dad assumed that the man in the truck was trying to catch his dog. So John pulled over to help him.

But the dog did **not** belong to the other man in the other truck - the dog was a stray, no tags, no collar. And even though they already have 2 dogs, John brought the dog home. As I looked at the dog I thought to myself : Where did he find water or food or a place to sleep away from coyotes and eagles?

This little dog had infected ears, the vet said, and is mostly deaf. It is completely blind in one eye and only some sight in the other due to cataracts. Nine teeth were gone and another 21 needed to be extracted. The matted, twisted fur needed to come off. The ominous question hung in the air when the vet asked John. "Are you going to keep this dog?"

John assured the vet that he was. Maggie had named him Oreo.

John & Shannon were prepared to give Oreo a chance at a better life ... through teeth extraction, neutering, surgical ear cleaning, and antibiotics ... through all of this ... Oreo had Maggie by his side ... with her tender-hearted protection.

After hearing about Oreo's recovery, I couldn't wait to meet him! I imagined napping with Oreo, on the sofa next to me, as I read a book. Taking Oreo for walks ... and playing with him like a new puppy. Little did I know that Oreo would eventually force me to take off my rose-colored glasses.

Each morning started with me walking Maggie to the school bus. As my day unfolded, I watched Oreo and petted him and made sure he got his fair share of food. I got fresh water in the bowl and carried him over to the bowl, so he knew it was full. I checked to see if he was near the swimming pool when he was outside. Due to poor sight he had only fallen in the pool once … and now his doggie GPS system seems to keep him back from the edge. He loved that I left the doors open all day; he and the other two dogs and the flies wandered in and out.

When I tried to take Oreo for a walk to smell some new smells- to step outside the yard – he pulled back, out of his collar – an automatic mistrust. And I saw a wariness that he had earned from life. And so I watched Oreo move through each day. But the truth is, Oreo only tolerated my attempts at friendship – he was indifferent to me … because I wasn't Maggie.

And then … at 3:40 in the afternoon when Maggie came home … Oreo would whimper and hop and whine as dog and girl were reunited … welcoming Maggie home .

And so I watched … watched Maggie and Oreo together … if we went shopping … when Mags returned, Oreo would whimper and hop and whine once again … if she watched television, Oreo curled up on the floor next to her … if Mags went to bed, Oreo was there, beside her. The two of them are tuned into each other like a radio signal that's crisp and clear… it's a private communication between them … a love that creates healing …

Oreo didn't need or want the whole world. He didn't ask to be a puppy again – he didn't ask for his sight or hearing back. He asked to be protected and cared for and have his needs met in a way that is right for him. So I began to look at Oreo with clear sight.

Maggie never asks him to be anything other than what he is ... a gentle soul who has suffered ... and he has everything now, that he needs now. A home ... a feeling of safety ... and a place to sleep each night ... right next to Maggie.

This Christmas wishing you ... the comfort of home.

Cathy and Joe

Overtime

6 13 2019

3M, a big successful manufacturing company, that frequently asks and even sometimes requires, weekend overtime. When this is going on, it's a big deal to take the whole weekend off! The compensation helps a lot too – time and a half for Saturdays and double time for holidays.

Robbie was going to take the entire weekend off! Just the thought of it was like a dog drooling over a T-bone steak. Rob was anticipating the leisure with Tom and Brittany and their playful kids were beckoning him to go swimming and fishing. He had some seniority now, and he was ready to take some play time! I couldn't wait to see him myself and I was happy for his well deserved time off.

Later that day I found out that Robbie was going to be working instead of coming to the lake.

I was stunned! I was disappointed. I wondered what in the world had happened to change his mind. Robbie is one of those fastidious employees who knows everything about the number of hours he has worked. So, I knew it wasn't a mathematical error. Something else had happened.

It was only later that I found out, the young man who was required to work that day, who had the least seniority, was going to be missing his child's birthday party ... unless someone else would work for him.

There you go ... What would you have done?

Robbie, the one with the big heart, couldn't possibly let that happen. He chose to work in his place ... on a weekend ... in the summertime,

3M is a big company and there's no time to notice someone who is about to miss their child's birthday. The policies are to keep the cogs of the corporate machine running smoothly. It's nice to know that there are people like Robbie who see beyond an employee number.

Things like this happen ... and are not reported in the news ... they're not even given a second thought, because it is that common. They happen over and over in every common ordinary day. All you have to do is notice ... notice the nice things that people do for each other ... and when you take a closer look ... at all the people at Aldi's that return their cart and leave the quarter for the next person ... notice when someone jogs to the door to open it for when your hands are full ... notice when an unknown neighbor plows the snow for you ... and the list goes on and on forever...

Welcome to the world ... of tiny keepsake moments. Noticing one after another ... after another ... after another ... leads you to the conclusion that you might not have anticipated.

Despite the television news ... see for yourself ... right in your own little world ... it's happening so frequently – so flawlessly ... that we don't even notice. Robbie's 'seniority' in the workplace was taking it to a higher level ... caring about an individual cog in the machine. A company that big can't care; they can't do that – but an individual can ... when you take the time to notice ... the real humanity in each person that surrounds you ... it teaches all of us to be more selfless ... even though we missed having Robbie there that day ... the money he earned came with a huge raise in a feeling of inner satisfaction ... not just for Rob; but for the young father who got to spend a birthday with his child ... because that father will someday ... do it for someone else ... guaranteed.

A Child is Born

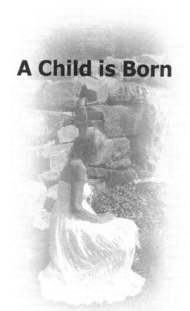

May 11th, 2017 3:30 PM 20 inches long 7 15 oz

I had security clearance to get into the room. Security code number for the room was 0047 ... the hospital room. The baby wore a security tag around his ankle that matched his mother's.

I was taking care of the house and the two little Yorkies while my son and his wife brought their firstborn child, Cameron, into the world. After they came home from the hospital, I willingly took the middle of the night shift to hold baby after his nursing was done, while the worn-out momma and daddy went back to bed.

I stared ... and hummed to the baby ... adoring every quiet still moment ... looking at each facial features ... hearing those infant squeaks that a newborn makes as they squirm and grow. I tried to stay awake to watch as the baby slept ... tried as hard as I could, but as I watched him breathing in and out in perfect rhythm, my own eyes closed, and I laid on the sofa as close to the edge as possible, to be near his little sleeping body without disrupting him.

A couple of days later I was packing to go home, and Tom came to ask if I might stay one more night. I was thrilled to be asked! I was more than willing to spend one more night awake in the quiet hours, holding this most precious newborn baby.

Days later I eagerly returned to their home with Grandpa Joe to meet Cameron for the first time. On the sofa Joe and I were huddling together creating a cocoon around Cameron as we passed him back and forth, looking him over, in the way that an animal examines their new young ... making sure that all was well.

I took Cam's little baby mittens off and said to Joe, "Did you see his little fingers?" The two of us listened to the tiny baby squeaks that came with every move he made.

As he laid trustingly in his grandpa's arms I asked Joe in a whisper, **"Did you know you could love this much?"**

I glanced over my shoulder at the new parents standing in the kitchen together. My son had his arm around his wife's waist ... they were **watching us** ... meet their firstborn child ... a new delivery from God ... in fresh and innocent terms ... a brand new start.

The first weeks passed, and the baby grew. I watched my son ... with his son. Cameron's baby toes were dipped in the chilly water, being held by his daddy, at their home on Wall Lake for the very first time ... a father/son ceremony of sorts ... on July 22, 2017. Sometimes I want to ask him; **"Did you know you could love this much?"**

I want to ask; Do you know that you are going to watch every step he takes ... for the rest of his life? ... out of sheer excitement watching him become himself.

Should I tell him that I am still watching him grow ... and I still ask myself all the time, **"Did you know you could love this much?"**

With my first child the answer was NO – I didn't know I could love that much. I didn't know that the children born to me would compel me to become the best version of myself, because I want to be my best for them.

I've seen Tom pick up baby Cameron, while at the same time Brittany reaches out her hands to take him and my son said softly, in a 'talking-to-baby-kind-of-way' "No, I wanna hold him."

They both want to hold him; right now there is only one, they have to share the miracle between the two of them, like sharing a delicious meal and there is just not enough to go around.

And in the future when there are more children ... the question will remain the same, **"Did you know you could love this much?**

But by the time the next child is on the way they will already know the secret of love. **The fact that love is ever expanding** ... that it **opens up** and **makes room for more**; more of everything ... more fun ... more room on your lap ... more room in your heart ... just more ... of everything good that you can't see!

This child being born has opened up a world of love for my son and his wife that will never stop expanding ... and I know ... I will never ask again, **"Did you know you could love this much?"**

Searching For Gabriel

December 22, 2019

Like the townspeople in the story following the Pied Piper ... I heard a sound that made me want to follow the notes. This was a violin, and I certainly didn't expect a live Christmas concert at Wal Mart!

I've never seen live entertainment of any kind in a Wal Mart. Last Fall I did see a young man with a pregnant wife, setting up a portable speaker in the Wal Mart parking lot. I made a mental note to give them a donation on my way out. But most likely someone asked them to leave because, by the time I left 20 minutes later, they were gone.

I walked by the young man who was playing a violin that had a cord attached to a speaker. It was heavenly ... so mellow ... so comforting ... it was like being serenaded. I wanted to stop and listen, but the heavy flow of Christmas shopping foot traffic carried me along with it.

I quickly gathered the few items that I needed and then followed the serenading sounds back to the center of the store. I looked over and saw a woman who appeared to be in her 80's, who had simply pulled her cart out of the nonstop flow of traffic and was listening to the young man's music. She was lost in the melody and didn't care who knew it. As if there were a parking spot just waiting for me, I gracefully backed my cart out of foot traffic into the space next to her. She was delighted that someone else, besides herself, had decided to stop and really listen to the young man.

She told me, she had asked one of the employees who the young man was and they said that he just came in and asked if he could play Christmas music for the people. And whomever he asked, had said yes. So, there he was, confined into a tiny space where you could hardly see him, tucked away with women's clothing surrounding him. He was just a few feet from the main aisle of non-stop shoppers and the long lines at checkout lanes. I found myself wondering, what miracle had happened that this young man was playing a violin so magically in the middle of a Wal-Mart store.

The woman told me that the young man had played "Mary Do You Know" and it was so incredibly beautiful!!!

I said "Really?"

"Yes" she said. She wondered out loud, "Do you think he would play it again?"

At first, I thought she wanted it played a second time for **me** to hear it. Then I realized that she wanted to hear it a second time, but was too shy to do the asking.

She was delighted that; I was willing to go over and ask the high school age musician to play it again. I dodged through foot traffic and crossed the shopping aisle freeway. Warmly putting my hand across his back, I quietly spoke closely into his ear. I told him that the woman over there said that he had played a song called "Mary Do You Know". He nodded his head in agreement. I asked him if he would be willing to play it again? With a smile of gratitude for the compliment, he heartily agreed.

So, the older woman and I stood side by side, listening to the music ... listening to the young man ... listening to the violin ... as people walked by as if they could see no one there at all ... She kept wishing that others would stop but they did not. She told me that she had given him some money and I knew that I would do the same before I left. None of the store employees were watching or even noticing our two small donations of money, right there inside the store.

The woman told me that the young girl standing off to the side was the performer's twin sister. His sister was thrilled that someone had finally STOPPED to listen to her brother play. She appeared to be his biggest fan.

The older woman next to me told me that she was 85 years old now and life experience has taught her to **stop** and listen to the music. She wanted the name of the young man and his address so that she could write him a thank you card and so his twin sister gave the woman the information. The woman told me that the young man's name was **Gabriel**. His twin sister was **Naomi**.

Wow! I thought to myself, those names really fit the season! No wonder somebody authorized this performance! How could you say NO to two people with those names? How could you say NO to Gabriel? I mean after all; Archangel Gabriel was the messenger sent to the Virgin Mary with the news that she would have a son.

I stayed a while longer ... enjoying the calm music in the middle of pandemonium and before leaving the store, I turned back to the 85-year-old woman, who was still listening, and asked what her first name was. She smiled coyly as if about to say something profound and said: **"EVANGELINE"**. I know my eyes got wide and my eyebrows lifted. I pushed my shopping cart out of the building in stunned silence. I was shaking my head. C'mon! Seriously????? You just can't make this up!

Now fascination and the mystery of it all were both rolling around in my brain! I was intrigued! I had to know more ... who was Gabriel? What High school student brings a violin and a speaker to Wal Mart and offers to play Christmas music? And what prompted store personnel to say YES to Gabriel?

Wishing I had asked for his contact information too, I needed to find Gabriel ... I was planning a holiday gathering and this young man would be the perfect entertainer ... all I had to do was find him. In small town America it should be easy.

I called the manager of Wal Mart ... certainly the general manager would have to authorize live entertainment ...

but it was obvious as we spoke that the manager had no idea what I was talking about ... nothing.

I called the music director of our local high school ... certainly this kind of talent must be known to the music director ... he too had never had a student named Gabriel nor anyone that fit the description who could play a violin as I described, he had no idea ... nothing.

I called the administration office at the main high school ... certainly a set of twins in a database – searching for uncommon names like Naomi and Gabriel would be an easy find ... nothing ... there was no Gabriel to be found.

As my mind kept going around and around trying to find answers and explanations ... I finally STOPPED and I heard that still small voice within ... almost an angelic voice in my head say:

"Read the lyrics!"

"What?" I asked inside myself.

The message was repeated more emphatically the second time: "Read. The. Lyrics."

It had never crossed my mind that the meaning of this experience was in the lyrics of the requested song. There I saw what should have been obvious.

The message ... yes from the Great Messenger Archangel Gabriel proclaiming good news of a miracle about to happen ... a child will be born ... a baffling miracle with a story that has been shared around the planet.

I had been searching for Young Gabriel because I couldn't believe that there was a miracle happening in Wal Mart? Why not? Maybe because Wal Mart seems an unlikely location for a miracle ... but so is a stable in Bethlehem an unlikely location ... and I wanted to know how all these pieces came together to create this moment just for me ... no one else saw what I saw that day – no one else asked the people's names ... no one else was standing next to Evangeline. I was bewildered until I read the lyrics.

Archangel Gabriel is the Great Messenger and Evangeline was the "bearer of good news." The two of them share a common purpose with one another. I could see it in her eyes; ... I could see it in her coy smile as she almost dared me to get the connection when she sweetly said that her name was "Evangeline."

Archangel Grabriel was directing a symphony of events ... a symphony designed for one person ... for Evangeline. Out of hundreds walking by ... one person stopped to listen to the young Gabriel ...

The Great Messenger Gabriel orchestrated every magical interaction that had to take place for her event to happen. The young Gabriel was there to serenade Evangeline with a song she got to hear TWICE, because of me.

Coincidence? Not a chance.
Miracle? Yes.
But **not my** miracle.

It was Evangeline's Christmas miracle and I got to watch it unfold ... I got to hear the tone of significance when she spoke Naomi and Gabriels names ... and the wonder in her voice when she said Gabriel just walked in and asked if he could play for the people ... I got see the sparkle of meaning in her eyes as she told me her name. She knew way before I did, she had a connection with Gabriel ...

both Gabriels ... the one playing the violin and the one directing her miracle.

I doubt that anyone else in the store saw or heard Gabriel that day. I should have known ... that this was a private concert ... designed just for her.

I was a stage hand ... helping out at the right time ... watching from the wings ... while the two Gabriels gave a stunning Christmas performance ... just for Evangeline ... right there in Wal Mart.

Gummy Worms

 Robbie Weber
★ Favorites · June 2 · 👥

This guy. My uncle. Had me convinced for years that the big fish on his wall was caught with a GUMMY WORM! Lol. I was totally sure of it. Even now as I write this, I feel like that's the story I want to believe. He was a wonderful uncle. Life has always been busy, but he would take the time to ask about your life. I learned too many things to count from this man. So today I'm going to go say goodbye. Then I'm going to head to the lake where some bright eyed kids call me uncle. I'm gonna bring a big bag of GUMMY worms. We'll eat most of them. But I'm gonna use a few as bait. Love you Uncle Sheldon!

After Sheldon's funeral Robbie posted these memories of Sheldon on Facebook with the stringer of fish.

Until reading my son's post, it had never occurred to me where Robbie had learned to be such an extravagantly wonderful uncle. Now I see it; the resemblance between Sheldon and Rob – not on a physical level ... but on an emotional level ... always making someone else smile. Always encouraging someone else. It's no easy task to follow in the footsteps of Sheldon.

A couple of days after the funeral, I set a tub of gummy worms into my shopping cart. I took a picture and sent it to Robbie, knowing that in Uncle Sheldon's honor, we would need more gummy worms this coming weekend.

The weekend, indeed, was filled with talk about Uncle Sheldon. The stories and the memories were endless. Can you REALLY catch the big one ... with a Gummy worm?

Uncle Sheldon was a master of letting that question hang in your mind. He was one of those guys that told the truth and you trusted him ... and that's how he set the hook with you ... and then he would reel you in just a little at a time by telling a whopper of a fish story!

I can just hear him saying, " Well, let me tell you" as he begins his story . " There was a time when I was out of bait – not a thing on the boat and all I had were those GUMMY WORMS in my flannel shirt pocket and I thought, "What the heck ... and I put one of those gummy worms on the hook; tossed it just to the edge of the weeds ... it was the end of the day and I was all by myself ... and I pulled in the biggest fish I EVER caught!"

And you knew for sure ... after hearing his story ... that if you were ever alone in a boat with no one else watching – without telling another single soul ... you just wanted to TRY it – for the hell of it – fishing with a GUMMY WORM ... so that one time – YOU could tell your story to a nephew or niece with the same SHIT-EATING SHELDON grin on your face ... about your big adventure with a Gummy worm and a fish.

Robbie has customized 'Sheldon's philosophy' and for him it fits with those four little wide-eyed kiddos that count on him ... he is with them often and is a constant presence and vital part of their lives.

Uncle Robbie is a big guy that spoils them and yet never stops coaching them to be their best self ...

They can count on their uncle Robbie and they trust him; he is there for them. No he does not change poopy diapers ... and that is about the only thing that he does not do. He is no stranger to bath time and potty chair reminders ... and endless hours of baiting hooks, untangling fishing line.

Like Uncle Sheldon was trusted, the kiddos trust every single thing Robbie says; and I wonder if there will be a time while the kiddos are still small ... when it's still believable ... that Robbie just might tell those kids that the big fish in the picture was caught with a GUMMY WORM ... or maybe he'll just tell the story – a fish tale ... about the fish that got away but was almost caught with a GUMMY WORM.

And now they believe and they wonder about the gummy worm story ... and they vow that some time when they are grown up and by themselves, with nobody watching, they are just going to try it ... because even as they grow into an adult ... that niggling little doubt ... still hangs around ... is it possible? ... that the story is true?

They know that they are going to carry the story forward in time ... it is too good not to share and let others ponder and spread ... the harmless tale of Gummy wonder.

And as Uncle Robbie grows older ... and he hears the chatter of the gummy worm tale still being passed down ... knowing that Uncle Robbie has taken good care of the tale, like passing down an heirloom ... an inheritance of love and laughter.

Then some night at the lake ... as the sun is setting ... I bet Robbie will raise a glass ... and give a silent toast to the uncle that was the master storyteller ... sending a salute to dear Uncle Sheldon ... who started it all.

Welcoming Taylor

3 13 2020

The day the world shut down.

That's what I call it. The day granddaughter Taylor was born. On the first day the hospital in Fargo would not allow visitors and was even questioning whether the upcoming baby's birth could be attended by the father.

The only thing that was certain was that Robbie and Joe and I had a job to do. We were entertaining two little children for a few days as their mother and father went out into that uncertain world to have a baby. All our plans for entertaining these two little ones were shut down. We had planned to play at the arcade at the mall ... to take trips to the thrift store to look for 'new' toys ... to travel to the grocery store and to get free popcorn as we shopped ... all of it meant to entertain two little munchkins and all of it was cancelled until further notice.

So, we did the best we could.

We brought out paint projects and stickers. We used the lower level of the house as our place to 'go to'. Getting the Fisher Price basketball hoop into the center of the room and running laps around the ping pong table that was there then ... making it up as we went along, pulling out old toys to distract our worries while entertaining the children at the same time.

As the days drug on we finally welcomed the new baby home. There was uncertainty and questions floating in the air – and there were no answers. This time when I left my son and his wife with a new baby and two other little ones – I had no idea when I would be back ... no idea when I would hold my new little Taylor again and when I would see them face to face.

We made family Zoom calls to support each other – doing what an entire nation was doing – trying to get by - trying to manage the uncertainty. I was personally feeling sorry for myself, not seeing our new little granddaughter.

Months later when we finally did get to see Taylor, live and in person, she was content and had been snuggled by parents and siblings and she had been welcomed into the world with love ... perhaps even better... than when the world had been a normal place to reside ... but I had been thinking she couldn't possibly be fine without me ... her grandmother! LOL

But it was the other way around ... I was the one that was **not** fine without being able to hold and snuggle her.

She was good! SHE WAS WRAPPED IN THE ARMS OF FAMILY – staying snug and peaceful with no awareness of the world around her.

Taylor was welcomed home in an old-fashioned sort of way. It was quiet ... uninterrupted ... like in days gone by. Just her immediate family ... surrounding her for the beginning of her life on Earth. The neighborhood stayed away -- friends stayed away -- the overflow of well-wishers bearing gifts stayed away ...

Maybe those first couple of months of uninterrupted love fostered the charming beauty of this child. She overflows with giggles and deep throaty laughter that comes from deep inside. She smiles with her whole face and her eyes sparkle almost every moment that they are open.

Maybe Taylor is exceptionally bright and beautiful, BECAUSE of the world shutting down.

Maybe those first two months, alone with two parents and two siblings that love her more than life itself ... maybe she was so infused with love, that it's like a fine oil that's been saturated with a flavor.

Taylor's flavor is happiness ... pure untainted happiness. It is in every cell of her body – and it shines brightly as a beacon ... just pointing the rest of us back to the place where happiness resides ... showing us where those deep belly laughs are coming from ... where the sparkles in her eyes are stored ... where the warehouse of love is located ... always there ... even when the world is shut down ... she clearly shows us ... that happiness ... is right there ... inside ourselves.

Post It Notes

The client's transformation was nothing short of astonishing! Two weeks ago, this client, was in the throes of intense anxiety. Now the look on her face was relaxed and at ease.

The client was so relaxed that this time she brought her 11-year-old daughter along to her hypnosis session and the little girl had a smart phone with a headset. The mother asked if her wide-eyed beautiful daughter could sit in the other reclining chair watching an electronic device as we did her session.

I was a little bit skeptical at first, thinking that the young child might interrupt the mother's hypnosis session. But as we reviewed the mother's progress, the little child was quite content and involved with her headphones on.

When we were ready to begin hypnosis, as usual, I pulled the blinds and put the blanket over the legs of the mother. The little girl paid no attention to the room darkening or the sound of background music in the room. As promised, she did not interrupt, not even once. She was glued to her device.

When the session was over, I took the blanket from the mother and playfully put it on top of the little girl. She laughed and smiled. She was still quite consumed by the electronic device in front of her.

I talked with my client about a follow up session and then I reached inside my desk drawer and pulled out several colorful packages of 3M Post-it notes.

The little girl was stunned as I started placing multiple packages of Post-it notes in her hands.

She put her phone down!

She took her audio headset off!

She put her device and headset in her mother's bag, so that she could carry the Post-it notes! She was giggling and giddy as she was mentally planning what she would do with the note pads and where she would hang her mini-artwork when she had created it. It was a delightful thing to watch!

A different day, a little 10-year-old client – a boy this time, was also in the office for anxiety; I gave him emoji and regular Post-it notes on his last appointment. His mother was scolding him and saying he was taking too many! He replied, "But mom! Her **whole drawer is full**!"

And he was right! My whole drawer WAS full!

I have an endless supply of these smile-producing sticky notes because my son willingly gets them from the 3M employee store at little cost – the items purchased there cannot be resold, they are for personal use only by the employee and their family.

Me? I personally use them as welcoming gifts and conversation starters for new people moving into our office building. I can't even count how many offices I have delivered free Post-it Notes to. I give them to little kids and big kids; everybody uses and loves post its.

Each Thursday the Caring and Sharing office delivers entire households of furniture to several families in need. And how do they designate which pieces of furniture are going to a particular household? Yep, with different colored Post it Notes. All the items with a blue sticky note go to one truck and all the items with a pink post its go to another truckload and on and on.

They were using this system long before I gave them post it's – I simply check with them from time to time to make sure this volunteer non-profit organization is well supplied.

And Robbie gets all the credit. My son Rob has a full life ... he could just blow it off; just let it slide and say it's not important enough for him to spend his time and money each week getting Post it notes from the company store to share ... but he loves my stories from people of all ages ... thanks to Rob I have had more than my fair share of fun!

It was a fun little game between Rob and I ... sort of like a shared venture that ties us together ... giving to others ... all about making the world go around...

But the Post-it note years are over now; Rob doesn't work at 3M anymore ... but it sure was fun while it lasted. It was like passing out bright colored cotton candy ... without the calories. From week to week I would share 'Post it note' stories with Rob in text message exchanges.

Maybe another mother and son TagTeam wouldn't find Post-it notes so entertaining, and maybe the two of us both ... just looked at the possibilities; 3M's manufacturing helps the world go around in a Big Way; it's a HUGE company!

And at the same time, its SMALL employee store at almost giveaway prices, gave Robbie and I the opportunity ... to bring color and FUN ... to the world ... in a small way,

I hope 3M is happy with what we did ... making people smile and helping out organizations that help the disadvantaged. They gave the two of us the opportunity to just run with it and see what we could do on a small scale ... not everything needs to be BIG ... we distributed smiles in a small way ... one or two or ten packs of Post-it notes at a time. Thank you 3M ... I loved that a little girl put her headphones and device down ... and chose the multicolored delight of Post-its notes instead!

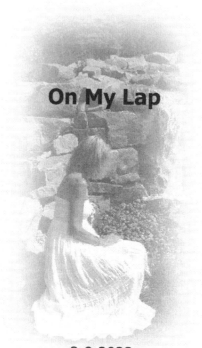

On My Lap

2 9 2022

People driving above 30 mph seemed to just find the ditch. As I got nearer to Fargo there were semi-trucks in the ditch – and lots of emergency flairs on the freeway blocking off areas. No serious accidents at all.

Those last ten miles of blowing snow, I was doubting myself; but there was no point in turning around and going home. I might as well keep on going and hope the roads would be better later this afternoon for my return trip home – or maybe I would stay the night – after all, there is a room designated for me – that makes me feel pretty dang important!

I texted ahead and asked to have someone open the garage door instead of using the front door. Pulling into the driveway, I saw the garage door lifting and three little children greeted me hollering, "Grandma! Do you need some help?"

Cam was wearing a jacket over pajamas with bare calves and on his feet were winter boots – Tatum had no socks and was wearing crocks and little Taylor was jumping up and down with excitement ... all of them had been pulled away from their breakfast to open that garage door and help grandma unload bags of preschooler projects!

The greeting by the kids in the garage was well worth the slow trip. So, what did we do that day?

After momma left to take some well-deserved time for herself, we played. Yes, we did!

The kids saw the giant Paw Patrol coloring pages and we were off to the races! It's grandma day! We sat on the floor and colored with crayons and markers. We did puzzle letters and brought out party favors that look like a snake unwinding when you blow into them. We printed our names and put stickers on a giant post-it note to put on the wall. We ran around downstairs in the basement and had lunch that momma had made ahead for us. We did a children's paint project and ... after lunch we made Banana peanut butter ice cream. Yes, they have to wear ear protection and they push the pulse button on the food processor. It was a whirlwind of nonstop activity in less than four hours and I loved every single minute.

Midday, Tommy sent me a message from his office, that the sun had come out and the roads were good now.

When it was time for their momma to return home, we were downstairs playing in a fort. I asked Cam and Tatum if they heard momma come home upstairs.

Cam said, "**Yes, but you can stay! You don't have to go home.**"

Then Tatum said "**You can't go home grandma! You have to sing songs and nibble ears before we can take a nap!**"

On the way home I asked myself why was this day with the children was so much more satisfying and delightful for me? Why did I feel so filled up ... even more than usual?

I realized that it is because at the start of the day, **Cameron wanted to sit on my lap** ...

because Cameron wanted to sit on my lap ... **Tatum wanted to sit on my lap ...**

because Tatum wanted to sit on my lap ... **Taylor wanted to sit on my lap.**

That was the magic ... lap time. I've seen it time and time again ... if I am eating a salad , the kids want a salad ... if I am eating an apple before bed — all of a sudden the three kids each have apples — and the same thing happened with lap time today — Cameron started it and they just kept rotating on and off my lap. For me it was blissful kissing their faces and holding them close as we moved through the day of activities.

I don't know when my sons outgrew my lap. I don't know when the time was over and they were too big for that ... but I'm wiser now ... I am not so busy now ... and I am paying closer attention now ... knowing ... that lap time becomes more valuable than gold .... it is short lived ... and I am going to capture it for the long haul.

Now that I know that it will end at some point ... I am going to store that feeling away ... because you don't get to have it from other people's children or grandchildren – it comes because you earn it ... it only comes with time and attention ... you can't just walk in one day and say 'hey little one, come and sit on my lap and let's snuggle'. It doesn't work that way ... you have to be there over and over and over again until they know with certainty ... you have **earned that lap time**. That is when a child truly sinks into your lap ... when they let their whole being sink into and meld with you ... that easy ... comfortable quiet ... sort of feeling ... THAT is the prize!

Maggie's World

"Maggie," I said to my granddaughter on Facetime, "Does it seem that the best part of your day is when you're with the special needs kids? They don't create drama like this."

On the other side of the screen she sat quietly and said sadly, "I know".

She had been telling me all the teenage drama that was going on at school. But her conversation about special needs people was at a completely different level; always at a level of realism and never drama.

Now that Maggie is done with high school she's working at an adult daycare facility for special needs adults. Her first day of work, Maggie met Miss Jackie, a special needs adult.

Miss Jackie immediately asked for a cup of coffee and Maggie willingly obliged. They went together to the kitchen to make a cup of coffee. Very soon Jackie asked again, "I'd really like another cup of coffee". Maggie willingly obliged.

Shortly after the second cup of coffee, Maggie was informed by a co-worker that the woman everybody calls Miss Jackie was allowed only **one** cup of coffee per day. Mags knew she had been duped... and laughed at herself and enjoyed the joke as much as Miss Jackie enjoyed it. Miss Jackie outsmarting Maggie on her first day, was topic of teasing conversation that night at home.

Mags told her parents they could see pictures from the daycare on Instagram. Almost every day they posted pictures at the care center when they were celebrating National Ice Cream Day - National Pajama Day - National Go Barefoot Day and the list goes on. Each evening Maggie told stories about the wonderful people and experiences.

Finally, out of curiosity, one evening Maggie's mom found the page of pictures on Instagram from the daycare. She stood there quietly for some time – just letting the pictures sink in - with tears welling up in her eyes, she called Maggie's dad over to see a picture of Miss Jackie.

Miss Jackie is black.

Let's just let that sentence hang there – all by itself – all alone – in the air - and go back and read it again. In weeks of working now, not once had my granddaughter with the long blond hair and pale white skin, ever mentioned that Miss Jackie's skin color is black.

That's because Maggie doesn't notice ... Maggie has never cared... and neither did I, until the television news brought color into my awareness.

I was exactly like that, when I was Maggie's age.

At 17 years old, I went to college. I was a freshman having supper with a group of new friends who were sophomores, when one young man stood up and said he had to go to a minorities meeting. In my Maggie-like innocence I said to him, "Why?" He splayed his hands down the front of his body as if to show me his skin color and he said, "Because I'm black???"He looked at me quizzically. Like, wondering if I really had not noticed.

Just like Maggie, I had not.

It is the media that has taught me to be scared ... other people have taught me to be scared ... scared I'm going to say something wrong. What if I look at someone the wrong way, and they don't interpret my motive in a positive way? What if they interpret my motive like the news?

One day at the office I was circling the block looking for a parking space. There was a young man who was walking on the sidewalk – yes he was black. I smiled and waved at him as I went by. Not finding a space to park I went around the block again – the young man on the sidewalk clearly was SCARED – of me! He glared at me as though I was harassing him! I couldn't believe that my greeting to him and the simple act of looking for a parking space had been misinterpreted.

To make matters worse, he ducked into my office building – most likely trying to get away from ME! What an unintentional mess! How could I stop him and tell him I meant no harm? Would he even believe me?

Just a few days ago I was leaving the office building using a set of outdoor steps that overlook the lake. The sun was shining brightly and a woman in glossy colored robes was sitting at the bottom of the steps, not knowing that I was coming down behind her – if I continued without speaking I was going to scare the crap out of her.

So I shouted out, "I'm coming from behind you!"

Again I repeated, "I'm coming from behind you! "

She stood up to let me pass by. I asked her if she had a child testing for a driver's license – she said yes – I placed my hand on her arm – the colorful robes that surrounded her face and body were gently swaying in the breeze. I asked her how old her child was. Most are testing at the age of 16 but hers was 26 … I asked if it was a boy or a girl – boy she said – then I told her what I tell every parent who has a child testing. She was hanging on every word I said.

"The examiners here are really nice!" I said to her " They are so friendly and they really want you child to pass … I just want you to know that". There was a sigh of relief that washed over her face as she returned to waiting. She was back into the parent posture, as I have come to think of it . That stance that says, "I'm waiting with baited breath".

I don't' know that woman's name and I have no idea where she was born. I don't know what God in the universe she worships.

But I'm with Maggie all the way ... it just doesn't matter to me. Race ... color ... spiritual belief ... the only thing Maggie really needed to know is that ... Miss Jackie only gets one cup of coffee a day.

Leave Wanting More

Hours of laughter and great conversation left a soft echo in my house after everyone left. I cried as Carol (my best childhood twin friend) and her granddaughter little Miss Annie left this morning. I cried because I wanted more.

Then I cried again when my brother Michael (my second-best childhood friend) and his wife Patty left. I cried because I wanted more.

In the deafening quiet, I sat on the steps of the front deck looking out at our farmland. I was analyzing the feelings of being left behind, and I guessed that the one who cries the most is the one left behind in the silent house.

But then I thought back to a time when I was the one leaving my mom and dad's house, watching as they stood outside on their porch, waiting for the final wave goodbye, as I drove out of their driveway. That time, I was the one **leaving** ... and I cried on the way home.

I cried because I had noticed my mom's hair turning gray that day. The change was so gentle and subtle that you could hardly see it happening. But still I knew, without a doubt, that time and life was moving forward without my permission.

Now, sitting there on the front porch steps this morning, pondering these thoughts, I realized that I can't win! I cry if I'm the one leaving, and if I'm the one being left behind. Both ways ... I **still wanted more**.

When I was a young girl growing up in the country, I **could not wait** to leave the country ... to explore TOWN and find NEW anything, and to live the life of my dreams. Now, in my day-to-day ordinary life, when I'm leaving town ... now at the end of the day, I can't wait to get home to the country. It doesn't matter if it's sunny or if it's a white carpet of snow on the ground, I can't wait to get to the sprawling wide-open space we get to call home.

When I was a young girl growing up in the country, my mom cooked and baked everything from scratch, and **I couldn't wait** to grow up and I swore I was going to buy and eat things from stores, delis, bakeries, and restaurants. Now, as I write I feel the comfort of my own oven warming the house and fragrances filled with my own creations. I wouldn't dream of buying a potato salad or rolls from the bakery.

When I was a young girl growing up in the country, I remember my mother being delighted over getting a box of free-range country eggs from a farmer. She was giddy, eyeing up the eggs that were brown or some green and some blue. I would see the smile on her face and her eyes sparkle; I just didn't get it!

Now, my husband brings free range country eggs from someone at work who raises chickens. I am giddy eyeing up the eggs that are brown or some green and some blue. I delight over every bright orange yolk inside my soft-boiled egg. Now I cannot tolerate a yellow yolk when I know that orange is available.

I am a completely different person than my mother was and yet I am the same. I want more of everything that is good and positive and powerful. That is my greed ... I'm not satisfied until good things are overflowing ... I love the country ... farm fresh eggs ... my hair graying gracefully like my mother's did ... what my mother has taught me ... and I love me and who I have become. I think I have chosen **the best parts of my mother to keep as my own.**

********4 25 2020*******

During the pandemic in April of 2020 granddaughter Maggie chose to stay home one weekend when John and Shannon were going to Flagstaff ... she was adamant that she wanted to be grown up; she was breaking out from dependance on her parents, and she wanted to stay home by herself.

She started to cry as her parents were leaving, and they offered her a way out ... telling her that she could pack up her things and come along! They would love to have her come along! But she stuck to her decision to be independent and stay home alone, and still she cried.

John put his arms around his grown-up baby girl and said, "You're just like your grandma, you have to cry when you say goodbye."

Later we were on Facetime and Maggie told me what my son had said to her and I remember thinking; "Oh my God Maggie! I hope so, Maggie! I hope you're just like me. I hope you **love life** and **people** and that you feel a **mountain of contentment** and you **love deeply** . And you see the wonder of the world every single day! And I seriously hope you love yourself as much as I LOVE YOU. I hope you **pick the BEST parts of me ... to keep.**

*******7 15 2022*******

They were out having a beer, John told me. After two beers John said to Shannon, "Let's go" in a very matter-of-fact way.

"Why?" she asked as she got up from her chair.

John replied "Because we always stay until we've had enough ... until we're tired of it ... and sometimes it's good to leave when you're wanting more."

*******7 16 2022**********

Joe and I were dancing at the Elks on Wall Lake. Rock with Dock Out had gotten relocated because of a massive downpour from the clouds up above, so the music had to move inside. The tiny dance floor was packed with all the sandbar partiers ... nobody cared that we were all cramped together and not spread out on the warm sand.

At the end of the night as the band started the last song, we were part of the dance floor frenzy that was gearing up to holler "One more song!! ONE MORE SONG!"

What John had said in our conversation the night before had landed in my mind and rang true ... I said to Joe in a matter-of-fact way, "Let's go ... let's leave wanting more ..." and we did.

****

I like that a lot – the tears over my twin sister as she was leaving ... the tears over my brother as he was leaving ... the tears when I used to be able to say goodbye to my parents ... the tears every time I say goodbye to my son at the airport ... my granddaughter Maggie being just like me ... yup I like that a lot ... because they are NOT tears of despair ... they are a celebration of feelings in liquid form. Tears; a liquid gift of connection with hidden messages. They are shouting, "You mean the world to me, and **I want more."**

These people are comfort in my life ... like a cat or a dog that nestles up alongside you on the couch ... it just plain feels good ... and sometimes you have to go take a pee and you interrupt the comfort ... and isn't that the tough part? When you disrupt the fun? But it makes it so much better when you come back – when you sink back into that chair and feel them snuggle close again. And you feel those people that you love so much just fill the space around you ...

I have tried for a very long time now to make time stand still ... like when my sons were growing up, and I organized my time and life to spend evenings free and available with them ... I had to admit even back then that there was no stopping time. So, I have decided to **savor more – like savoring** these stories ... each little keepsake moment of wanting more is a reminder of something to **savor** in life ... from a single beer together ... to one final dance together.

There is never going to be enough time for my best-loved people; they are the greatest part of my life ... So, I will savor each moment with them and I will cry each and every time they leave ... or every time I leave them ... because I am certain ... I will **leave wanting more.**

Like Father, Like Son

It's wasn't an argument – really it wasn't! It was just two full grown men, each with a beautiful wife and four tickets to a concert – what trouble could they possibly get into?

While the wives were getting beautiful for the concert, Tom and Ben went to buy appetizers at a restaurant. Ben knew that after the concert ... 1 AM was going to arrive and find them hungry; they prepared by picking up appetizers cooked and boxed to bring home.

As they waited at the restaurant for their order, a great idea landed in their brains! They could upgrade their seats for the concert ... like kids, searching for the very best toy!!! Without consulting their wives they found premium seats that were a little bit more costly ... just a smidge ... well I don't actually know how much the tickets were – they might have been extravagantly expensive.

They put the appetizers in the frig and informed their brides that they had upgraded their seats! The guys were smiling and chuckling like cats that had eaten the canary. It appeared by their sheepish grins that they knew the upgrade was not necessary and somehow, they needed to sell this upgrade to their wives.

Their two stunningly beautiful brides were arguing with them. The tickets were more expensive – too expensive – the original purchase was good enough.

Remember, I was just an outsider; the grandma babysitter, watching from the sidelines. I have no side bets and no interest in who wins. I'm simply waiting for the adults to leave.

The grandkids know that I am NOT bringing out my Mary Poppins magic bag of games and activities, until the adults are gone. So, the kids and I are just watching as if it were a delightful sporting event going on in front of us. Husbands on one side – wives on the other - while the kids and I watch the conversation ball being lobbed back and forth across the net.

My experience with relationships makes it almost impossible for me to keep the belly laughs quiet! The children don't know what has tickled me to the point of near hysterical laughter. I can't help it! I'm trying not to laugh.

I ask the two ladies, "Why would you debate with two men who have mastered the art of sales?" I want to ask their young wives "Do you know what they do for a living!?! Do you realize they are going to **win** this conversation?"

This bantering was like watching a boxing match between a little child and the heavy weight champion of the world ... the campion just putting his gloved hand on the forehead of the little kid and letting the kid flail about harmlessly. It was all in good fun.

All four of them know that this is a first world issue ... they know how fortunate they are to be able to buy a better seat at a concert or to buy a seat at all! If this is the worst thing the two guys ever do, to upgrade seats at a concert ... well, that is forgivable.

What I loved most was the boyish grins on both of the guys faces ... they knew they were going to be scolded ... and they knew they were going to be forgiven ... and they had used the subtle art of persuasion.

I have watched these four adults together before – and these two men would NEVER disregard what their wives thought if there was anything larger at stake than a few dollars. I have seen and know how much they both love and respect their wives. And so, I laughed!!!! Upgrading tickets was just a little thing.

****

The water sprinkler was on in the front yard and little five-year-old Cameron wanted to run through that water in the heat of the summer. Just minutes ago, as his parents were leaving for a concert. Cam's mom shut the sprinkler off in their yard. Cam was **told by his mother** that she would be getting the water slide out tomorrow and that he **was not going in the water** tonight.

After his parents left, Cameron kept watching the neighbors now, setting up their sprinkler just a few feet away. The water coming so close to Cam's yard you could see that the little guy could hardly stand the temptation.

Cameron kept getting closer to the edge of the water drops on the grass. He was trying to convince me that he should put on swim trunks so that he can run in the water sprinkler. Over and over he kept asking. I had said NO several times.

Now that his parents were gone, and I was in charge – the subtle art of persuasion came into full form. Like father - like son, five-year-old Cameron came to me negotiating now , "We are taking a bath tonight right?" (Sales pitch here)

I said, "Yes you are taking a bath in just a few minutes!"

And with his head cocked just a little bit to the side, sort of like the way his dad looked at that age, he said to me "Then it would be OK for me to get my clothes wet in the water sprinkler, right?" (Sales pitch again)

And I said, "No it would not! Your mother said you are not going in the water sprinkler tonight!"

I was wondering if Cameron was going to go ahead and just run through the sprinkler anyway. When we finally went inside for bath time, Cameron's clothes were on and still dry – although he tried his best to persuade me otherwise.

Cameron was watching the playfulness tonight and the feeling of a little clash all in good fun and he is learning every step of the way.

Ben's son is an infant right now and too small yet to learn like Cameron did tonight, but it is coming soon. These sons are going to walk in their daddy's footsteps and I hope they are just like their daddies ... because underneath that sheepish grin of those two men tonight, is the knowledge that they have earned it. They have worked and worked hard ... they deserved the sheepish grin, they deserved the better seats, and they deserved to have time off to take a break and play at a concert.

The two of them have values that are rock bottom solid ... in business ... in parenting ... and as loving husbands. Occasionally they wear a sheepish grin and buy something that they know their wives might not agree with. And is that so bad?

At 1 AM after the concert the lighthearted debate was still going on as they pulled the appetizers out of the frig and warmed them up. Tom and Ben were still laughing, now not even trying to hide it, saying to the ladies "you have to admit these were good seats!"

Tom and Ben's sons are watching every day as they grow; they are watching two men with women who love them deeply ...   two women with husbands that return that love ... they are watching four parents who love their children ... four adults who are all beyond grateful ... that the biggest thing in the world they had to be bantering about ... was the price of concert tickets.

The Tree

The tree and I met seven years ago.

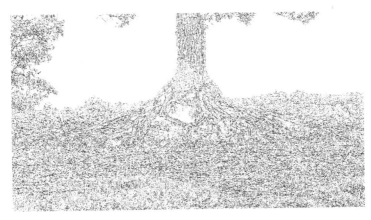

I was captivated by it the very first time I saw it. So much of it was exposed and its imminent demise made me think of an inmate on death row. I wondered how long it had to live.

Every two weeks, I had occasion to drive by the barnyard with the tree and the uncovered roots. I would see the cattle laying there using the exposed roots as a backrest and enjoying the shade.

The roots had been trampled, while the urine and manure and the rain wore away the dirt day after day. Maybe the tree was going to live longer than I thought. After all, the roots were locked tight down into the ground. I admired how the tree stood, and how it tolerated it all, hanging on so tight and so long down into the Earth.

One day as I was driving by, the cattle were meandering elsewhere, and the sun was shining. So, I stopped to take its picture. No one came by on the quiet country road. Nobody saw me taking pictures of a barnyard tree. Even though the roots were naked and exposed, the tree didn't seem to mind that I was taking photographs.

I snapped the photos quickly and later that day, on my large computer screen, I really examined the tree. It was like using a set of binoculars to look at the roots all tangled together like ropes, as I magnified the details for a closer look.

The hollow openings in the roots fascinated me. There is something so stunning about seeing what normally is hidden. Those roots were put down and growing strong way before the tree ever had a notion of what was to come. Its roots were establishing its strength without knowing that one day it would need every ounce of depth it had created ... just to hang on now ... one more summer ... one more season ... through one more storm.

I would've liked to have sat down in the hollow of those roots and looked out from the perspective of the cattle that lay underneath it. This tree was being useful. Everything about it was useful. It had become skin and bones by fulfilling its mission – by protecting the cattle as best it could until the day would come ... when it could not. There was no pretending that it was anything but an ordinary tree that was dying.

It just happened to be growing in a barnyard. No fairy tale stories of a Hobbit or a forest like Lord of the Rings.

It was not a famous celebrity like the giant sequoia General Sherman in California with 2.4 million visitors each year ... and yet this tree has me writing about it ... this tree captured my attention.

Just weeks after I took this photo, I drove by the tree and the top has broken off. I gasped when I saw it! There was space in the sky where the light flowed through ... where the tree used to be.

Someone had already hauled the top half of the tree away, and all that remained was the jagged broken off stump about six feet off the ground. I sat there on the quiet country road and gave a few moments of honor to the tree that had lived a hard but good life. I had known that the tree was dying and still it caught me off guard.

Two weeks later I came back and saw it again. By now the farmer had taken equipment and removed the roots of the tree. I sighed as I sat on the side of the road ...

I felt a kinship to the tree. As if by me watching it, it was being recognized and honored. The **cattle knew** what the tree had given them. How could they not? Their life was completely intertwined with the tree. The tree gave everything ... all of its time and life. The tree was going WITH the flow of life ... and in return the tree received a REASON to hang on ... a purpose that was bigger than itself.

Now the tree was gone; used up.

I have only known the tree for seven years but I had watched it provide an invaluable gift for the animals and get progressively weaker until one day it died; having been used up completely. It was used up ... and now it was gone...

****

I called Joe on his cell out in his shop, and I said, 'Have you seen the driveway?'

He said "WHAT?"

I said " Seriously, have you seen the driveway?"

It was a hot August night in 2022. Joe and I had taken a refreshing swim in Lake Ida. When we got home I took a quick bath and got out of the tub ... looking out the window to the driveway was ... a tree.

On a beautiful 85 degree day – not a cloud in the sky - no wind – full sun ... completely out of nowhere ... just five minutes after we had driven up the driveway, there lay a full grown tree that had simply toppled over and was covering our driveway.

Into the cell phone I said to Joe, "I will meet you in the driveway".

I met Joe outside and the two of us walked halfway down our driveway ... to a fallen tree ... that looked completely strong and green as it laid there. Sigh!

Seven years I had watched the barnyard tree get used up and break and fall, leaving this Earth without fanfare as it finally succumbed to years of hard work ... and now simply driving by a fully alive and grown tree that broke in half and fell right onto the driveway.

The two trees came down within days of each other, leaving me stunned at the contrast. One tree intrigued me by the depth of its roots and its ability to hang on ... to live long ... and get completely used up ... and the other coming down in the relative youth of its lifespan ... at an inconceivable time ... with no storms at all.

It's a mystery why a tree like that - that seems strong and healthy falls without reason and another tree is obviously used up fully ... I don't' have an answer ...

Maybe that's why it's called the Tree of Life, because life is an ongoing impromptu journey. The trees leave behind the good it has done each in their own way ... for the Earth ... for the people ... for the animals ... for the balance of the earth ... all parts being grateful that each tree gave something different to fulfill its own cycle.

Neither tree-of-life was better than the other – just different and fulfilled ... each life lived fully ... in their own natural way. Both trees surrendered to the life process that they were destined to have ... and when that life was over they each gracefully were welcomed back to the Earth in a different form.

As I look off into the future of those two trees and I can imagine that there is a day with neighbors and friends coming together ... just having a glass of wine ... and perhaps on the kitchen countertop there is a charcuterie board newly made from **old** wood, with sliced meat and crackers and olives immaculately arranged there ... and maybe beside it there is a cheese board with a slicer blade made from **young** wood ... and just maybe those two trees are side by side on that countertop, both of them having a new job in a much classier neighborhood.

Now the trees are living a new life and looking great ... a time of being on display ... no one knowing their history or ancestry ... no one knowing their hard times and the storms of their lives ... but the trees know what they have gone through ... now they have time to become friends ... continuing their journey ... side by side ... without anyone even noticing.

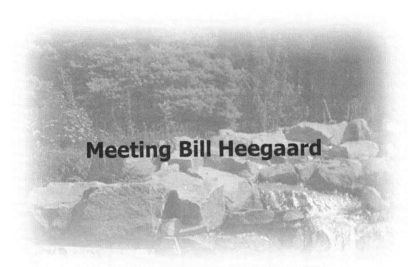

Meeting Bill Heegaard

I had no idea, that in the decades ahead both my baby and I would love this doctor. Walking out of the Emergency Room that night, my second baby boy, Robbie, just days old, had a lump the shape of an egg on his head.

The doctor delivering my precious son had told me that the egg was from pressure as he was trying to be born. He was a big one – almost ten pounds and trying to get born into the world had caused this ... the doctor had said it will go away with time and he will 'grow into it'.

The problem was, that every single person who met our new son, voiced their concern about the egg on his head. Over and over and over again other people voiced their distress about the well-being of the baby.

Finally, buckling under the fear and worry from others, we took Robbie to the emergency room only days after he had been born. I carried my newborn 'big baby' around the exam room as we waited for the doctor.

The doctor was courteous and examined my baby carefully, then said "This is simply from pressure during the birth process. It will go away with time, and he will grow out of it. He is just fine!"

I was resisting his words of comfort. I stood there looking dumbly at the doctor – finally he said, "Well, that's what you wanted to hear right!?!"

"Yes", I stammered as he left the room.

All of my non-medical friends had given me their doomsday predictions and fear … I had been convinced that they were right. I left and went home with my baby, not knowing that my baby and I would both grow up and come to know this doctor on a personal basis some 40 years later.

****

It may seem strange to greet a close friend using both first and last name – but Bill started it. He liked my hyphenated last name, so each time he greeted me he said, "Well hello Cathy Weber-Zunker; How are you?" and I would reply "I am fine Bill Heegaard. How are you?" This continued through our entire friendship.

I was the third person to help Josie Heegaard write her memoir … and the only one who had the pleasure of finalizing it. Josie didn't need my help writing – she just needed my eyes. Macular degeneration was not going to stop this lady! This marvelous woman in her 80's postponed having the memoir printed. Each time it was delayed, I sensed that she thought when the memoir was printed it would mean that her life was over!

When Dr. Bill Heegaard, her lifelong partner, and the love of her life, was sick in the hospital, I took the matter into my own hands. If this memoir didn't get printed soon, it was possible that one of them would die without seeing their life story in print. Without asking, I ordered proof copies and delivered them to Bill and Josie after Bill was home from the hospital.

I can still see the dumbfounded look on his face, almost unable to speak as he flipped through 450 pages of photos and stories. All the way through their courtship to the year they spent working with refugees in Thailand, and on to the current day.

I asked him, "Well, what do you think we have been doing every Thursday morning for the past 7 years?" He quietly looked through the book with pride and admiration. So thrilled that Josie had taken this in hand, despite her severely weakened eyesight.

Even with her eyesight waning, Josie was grateful for everything. Bill and Josie were the inventers of gratitude ... well... maybe they didn't create gratitude ... but this is where I saw gratitude expressed the most in real time.

As Josie laid on the love seat sofa off to the side of the kitchen, taking a nap, with a smile on her face, Bill would say to her, "You are so beautiful!"

She would smile back to him and say; "Aren't we lucky?"

"Aren't we lucky?" has become an everyday comment in our house because of Bill and Josie. We say it all the time.

****

One day when I was at Bill and Josie's home, I looked at Bill and I remembered ... it seemed to be the tone of his voice that triggered the memory that was lurking there in the back of my mind. I realized that Bill was the doctor I had met decades ago ... the one that I had placed my newborn son, Robbie, in his hands. He had been right all those years ago ... the baby was gong to be just fine! And yes, that was what I wanted to hear!

Robbie, as an adult pulling the pieces of his life together, moved back to Alexandria. Back then, he rode a bike back and forth to work each day and besides his regular job, he was looking for extra work and income. I said "Bill and Josie need someone to do odd jobs and yard work".

During this rebuilding time in Rob's life he wore out TWO bikes – completely used up, without the possibility of repair. One of those times when a bike died, happened while working at Bill and Josies' house. It was Bill who drove him to Wal Mart to buy a new bike and returned him home again.

****

One day I asked Bill "Could you look at my toe?" He listened to my tale of banging my foot on the freezer in the basement. The same voice of compassion from decades earlier said, "Well Cathy, I would love to look at your toe".

As he looked at my toes and moved them back and forth, he spoke words of comfort once again. I looked at him with new eyes. I saw that Josie's knight in shining armor had become dear to me too ... his gentle nature ... this man who loved Josie more than life itself. Because I was helping Josie be her best self in those last years, he loved me for that ... I could be her eyes as she wrote the stories of their life.

Bill loves ... the people that Josie loves.

Josie loves ... the people that Bill loves.

Theirs was a mandate; you couldn't love Josie without Bill and vice versa. There was no '**one** without the **other**.' It was a connection so powerful, that even the rest of the world saw it. Bill and Josie taught me about love and gratitude way more than I could learn in a book or a church ... they lived it and breathed it.

It's not until now, that I see the magic of my son being back with Bill Heegaard three decades after his birth. Bill watched in the background as Rob became his best self ... Bill spreading his own kind of medicine called optimism.

And now, after Bill and Josie are both gone, that legacy of hopefulness and healing, that they planted in their property is coming into full bloom! Now MANY will come here to become their BEST SELF.

All around Bill and Josie's home ... a campus is appearing ... as if it were sprouting one building after another! A Teen Challenge Campus will assist people in gaining freedom from chemical addictions and other life problems.

When the campus is finished, there will be a steady stream of people coming and going. There will be those saying that their wound is too big and will *never* heal ... many people who thought they had something insurmountable in their life ... until they come here to Bill and Josie's property ... where healing and optimism has been seeded into the soil ... and those gaping wounds that people thought would never heal, begin to scab over.

How could they not heal?

The land has been fertilized with hope ... and the lake whispers gratitude. So that if there is ever a voice of DOUBT or FEAR that starts sprouting in someone's head ... Bill's soothing voice of optimism will softly murmur ... "You're going to be just fine ... that's what you wanted to hear right?"

Writing in Stone

Story permissions:

Substitutions: permission from Maggie Weber

Like a good Neighbor – permission Tom Weber State Farm Agent

Cookies – permission Robert Weber

Laura My Bunny Lady – permission granted by Laura

Red Car- Permission granted Robert Weber

Rebecca – permission granted John M. Weber

Uncle Sheldon – permission my Jean Neis

Sara Wagner -- the photographer that sees through the lens of love. Permission granted for photo reprinting. www.smphotography.info

Mr. Swanson – permission granted by John M Weber

Hugging John - Paula at John's office

'God in my Office' – thank you Tina

Cover Design – thank you Carlos

Made in the USA
Columbia, SC
19 December 2023